OAE

Educational Leadership Practice Questions

Mometrix

TEST PREPARATION

Dear Future Exam Success Story

First of all, **THANK YOU** for purchasing Mometrix study materials!

Second, congratulations! You are one of the few determined test-takers who are committed to doing whatever it takes to excel on your exam. **You have come to the right place.** We developed these practice tests with one goal in mind: to deliver you the best possible approximation of the questions you will see on test day.

Standardized testing is one of the biggest obstacles on your road to success, which only increases the importance of doing well in the high-pressure, high-stakes environment of test day. Your results on this test could have a significant impact on your future, and these practice tests will give you the repetitions you need to build your familiarity and confidence with the test content and format to help you achieve your full potential on test day.

Your success is our success

We would love to hear from you! If you would like to share the story of your exam success or if you have any questions or comments in regard to our products, please contact us at **800-673-8175** or **support@mometrix.com**.

Thanks again for your business and we wish you continued success!

Sincerely,
The Mometrix Test Preparation Team

Copyright © 2026 by Mometrix Media LLC. All rights reserved.
Printed in the United States of America

Table of Contents

Copyright © Mometrix Media. You have been licensed one copy of this document for personal use only. Any other reproduction or redistribution is strictly prohibited. All rights reserved.
This content is provided for test preparation purposes only and does not imply an endorsement by Mometrix of any particular political, scientific, or religious point of view.

Practice Test #1

Multiple Choice Questions

1. A school leader wants to enlist support for change on campus. Which of the following actions should be taken first?

a. Communicate the intended change effectively to all stakeholders.
b. Create an advisory committee.
c. Find supporters with influence over other stakeholders to help spread the word about the change.
d. Administer an anonymous survey to see how stakeholders feel about the proposed change.

2. Which of the following best describes what school leaders should consider when identifying professional development for staff?

a. Individual staff members' goals are most important.
b. School goals and vision always take precedence.
c. Individual staff member and school goals are of equal importance.
d. Professional development is primarily for accountability purposes and goals.

3. Which of the following actions would be most effective for ensuring that shared vision and goals are implemented consistently?

a. Publishing regular updates regarding goal progress in the school newsletter and on the school website
b. Identifying barriers and challenges to vision implementation as quickly as possible and revising plans to address them
c. Delegating responsibility to others to assist with vision implementation, monitoring goal progress regularly, and holding all staff members accountable for fulfilling their roles in the implementation plan
d. Meeting regularly with internal and external stakeholders to solicit feedback and ideas regarding vision and goal implementation

4. Which of the following strategies most accurately identifies the school leader's role in implementing professional development?

a. Staff development is the sole responsibility of the school leader.
b. A school leader should delegate the implementation of professional development to the administrative team.
c. A school leader should leverage teacher leaders in the implementation of professional development.
d. School leaders are directly responsible for implementing professional development but should utilize their administrative team and teacher leaders where appropriate.

5. Which of the following is true regarding best practices for school leaders when giving teachers observational feedback?

a. Leaders should give feedback statements rather than asking questions.
b. Leaders should disregard strengths to focus on improving weaknesses.
c. Leaders should emphasize all identified areas for improvement equally.
d. Leaders should include some specific next steps attainable for teachers.

Copyright © Mometrix Media. You have been licensed one copy of this document for personal use only. Any other reproduction or redistribution is strictly prohibited. All rights reserved.
This content is provided for test preparation purposes only and does not imply an endorsement by Mometrix of any particular political, scientific, or religious point of view.

Refer to the following for question 6:

An assistant principal analyzes student performance data for the grading period and notices that a class of students consistently performs well in reading and has not demonstrated growth. The assistant principal is growing increasingly concerned about the quality of learning on campus.

6. Which of the following would be the best source of data for the principal to examine next?

a. Student survey data
b. Teacher survey data
c. Classroom observation data
d. Class size and student to teacher ratios

7. The dean of instruction conducted a classroom observation of a seventh-grade math teacher and noticed that the math teacher was not following the curriculum for the math department. When asked, the math teacher informed the dean that the students were not ready for the standards identified in the curriculum and that he chose to review standards from sixth- grade instead.

Which of the following would be the best response from the dean to the math teacher?

a. Commend the math teacher for addressing the gaps in student learning.
b. Require that the math teacher attend training on the math curriculum.
c. Model instruction of the standards outlined in the curriculum.
d. Direct the math teacher to teach the standards outlined in the curriculum.

8. Which of the following have education researchers identified as important regarding implementation of school-wide data initiatives??

a. More training opportunities and promotion of the data system in implementation are most effective.
b. Technology that supports data initiatives offers the answer to data use in schools.
c. Individual teachers utilize data technology systems more quickly and productively.
d. The success of a school data initiative is determined by the data system selected.

9. Which of the following statements correctly reflects considerations for school leaders in supporting school improvement through effective resource management?

a. The school vision and goals are most dependent upon physical resources.
b. Material resources are priority as they are needed for a safe, comfortable teaching and learning environment.
c. Fiscal resource management is necessary for managing other resources, with some exceptions.
d. Human resource management is necessary for smaller class sizes and optimal student learning and achievement.

Copyright © Mometrix Media. You have been licensed one copy of this document for personal use only. Any other reproduction or redistribution is strictly prohibited. All rights reserved.
This content is provided for test preparation purposes only and does not imply an endorsement by Mometrix of any particular political, scientific, or religious point of view.

10. For the third subsequent year, a school leader has had 40 percent turnover of teaching staff. This high rate of turnover has impacted the campus negatively and the school leader wants to address this concern. In a stakeholder meeting, the leader asks members to brainstorm suggestions for addressing teacher retention. Which of the following suggestions should the school leader implement first?

a. Administer a survey to teachers to get their feedback on what they like and dislike about working at the campus.
b. Petition the district to raise teacher salaries.
c. Offer bonuses to teachers who produce good student performance results on standardized assessments.
d. Provide mentors to new teachers on campus.

11. On which of the following do the Individuals with Disabilities Education Act and the Family Education Rights and Privacy Act differ with respect to student records?

a. Requiring instruction and training of educators on records confidentiality
b. Defining which student records are considered to be educational records
c. Determining conditions for destroying educational records via state laws
d. Regulating records collection, maintenance, confidentiality, or disclosure

12. How can school leaders problem-solve and plan for best allocating monetary and material resources to realize school goals for students in economically challenging times?

a. By postponing school improvements to a future date
b. By making cuts in funds allocated to student services and programs
c. By ending programs identified as not helping student performance
d. By eliminating professional development opportunities

13. Which of the following would most impact the success of a new teacher induction program?

a. Providing optional coaching sessions for new teachers
b. Assigning mentors to new teachers based on the seniority of the mentor teacher
c. Providing opportunities for collaboration and leadership development
d. The school leader facilitates all aspects of the induction program

14. Which of the following actions best demonstrates that a school leader is open to changing positions on an issue?

a. The school leader lets staff vote on decisions.
b. The school leader has an advisory committee made up of teachers, students, and community members.
c. The school leader holds regular community meetings to provide updates on school activities.
d. The school leader makes time to take phone calls from parents outside of school hours.

15. Which of the following most correctly represents criteria requiring a school to hold a Manifestation Determination Review for a student who receives special education services?

a. The school seeks a discipline-related placement change for more than 10 days in a row.
b. The school suspends a student on a one-time basis for 10 or fewer consecutive days.
c. The school suspends a student for 10 or more days in a school year for any reason.
d. The school creates or revises a behavior intervention plan.

Copyright © Mometrix Media. You have been licensed one copy of this document for personal use only. Any other reproduction or redistribution is strictly prohibited. All rights reserved.
This content is provided for test preparation purposes only and does not imply an endorsement by Mometrix of any particular political, scientific, or religious point of view.

16. During the annual summer meeting, the math department chair expresses concern that the math teachers do not have enough collaborative time to plan lessons and discuss student performance. Which of the following solutions would best address the department chair's concern?

a. Make adjustments to the master schedule to allot collaborative planning time for the math department.
b. Offer extra duty pay for math teachers to stay after school and plan together.
c. Purchase a technology platform that will allow the teachers to communicate asynchronously online.
d. Place substitute teachers in the math classrooms monthly to allow teachers time to plan together.

17. Which of the following statements is true about a school climate in which students feel supported?

a. Students find resources and support are readily available to them.
b. Students who share multiple classes are more likely to form relationships with one another.
c. Student roles and responsibilities are clearly defined in policy handbooks.
d. Student feelings of support are not affected by interactions with adults.

18. Which of the following is the best evidence of clear and effective communication regarding the school vision and goals?

a. Stakeholders who understand the vision and goals can articulate them in their own words.
b. Stakeholders can memorize the school vision and goals.
c. Stakeholders offer suggestions for revision of the school vision and goals.
d. Stakeholders support the school vision and goals.

19. Which of the following categories represents the highest percentage of budgetary expenditures for public schools?

a. Student support services
b. Operations
c. Instruction and instruction related
d. Administration

20. In terms of assessment, which of the following is a true statement that school leaders should consider when minimizing bias and maximizing equity for all students?

a. Accommodations given to students during testing are inherently unfair.
b. Progress monitoring using student data decreases achievement gaps.
c. Achievement gaps can be resolved by testing low performing students frequently and extensively.
d. Assessment validity and reliability nullifies most non-standardized test results.

21. Which of the following laws dictates how student information can be used in an educational setting?

a. HIPAA
b. FERPA
c. NCLB
d. ESSA

Copyright © Mometrix Media. You have been licensed one copy of this document for personal use only. Any other reproduction or redistribution is strictly prohibited. All rights reserved.
This content is provided for test preparation purposes only and does not imply an endorsement by Mometrix of any particular political, scientific, or religious point of view.

22. The dean of students informs the school principal that discipline data shows that a disproportionate number of black students have been suspended from school for the first semester when compared to the general population of students. Which of the following represents the best action that the principal could take?

a. Identify a mentoring program for black students on campus.
b. Assess the school culture to determine if there are negative assumptions or beliefs that impact teaching and learning.
c. Send an email to teachers that no black students can be suspended for the second semester.
d. Identify teachers who should attend classroom management training.

23. Which of the following best describes the relationship between the school principal and the school board?

a. The school principal recommends the hiring and termination of teachers to the school board.
b. The school principal reports campus data to the school board at board meetings.
c. The school board elects or hires and supervises the superintendent, who in turns hires and supervises the school principal.
d. The school board implements state and local policies that the principal must abide by.

24. A goal for XYZ High School is to increase teachers' and students' technology skills. Which of the following decisions best demonstrates that the leader is aligning resources to achieve the goal?

a. Require all staff communications to be paperless.
b. Purchase updated computers for teachers and students and provide training for using them.
c. Conduct regular professional development for teachers related to technology skills.
d. Offer a new course to students that teaches basic computer skills.

25. A school leader has recently been appointed to school principal of ABC Elementary School. Which of the following actions would best help the new principal learn more about the community that the school serves?

a. Research the community online.
b. Review student demographic and academic performance data.
c. Meet with a variety of stakeholders of the community.
d. Meet with current staff to ask questions about the community.

26. Which of the following barriers would interfere the most with achieving a goal of increased student achievement in math?

a. A shortage of calculators
b. A lack of community support
c. The adoption of a new math textbook
d. The unexpected resignation of a math teacher

27. Which of the following should be considered first when adopting curriculum?

a. Alignment to federal and state standards
b. Teacher approval
c. Community approval
d. Board approval

Copyright © Mometrix Media. You have been licensed one copy of this document for personal use only. Any other reproduction or redistribution is strictly prohibited. All rights reserved.
This content is provided for test preparation purposes only and does not imply an endorsement by Mometrix of any particular political, scientific, or religious point of view.

28. Which of the following is an effective way to use community resources to support student learning?

a. Invite local churches to host a back-to-school drive to provide students with school supplies.
b. Partner with local businesses to provide free tutoring to students after school.
c. Partner with local businesses to host field trips for students.
d. Invite local businesspersons in the community to mentor students.

29. Which of the following situations represents an issue of ethics?

a. The football coach obtained a sponsorship from a local restaurant to provide snacks for students during football practice.
b. A group of students make a request to form a club for students who were adopted.
c. The debate sponsor uses money collected from students for fees to pay for his lunch but replaces the money after school.
d. A pastor from a local church donates table linens to the drama department for an upcoming banquet.

30. During a classroom observation, a school leader notices that a student is sitting in the corner of the classroom and is not engaged in the lesson. The teacher does not attempt to engage the student during the lesson. When the school leader meets with the teacher about the observation and asks about the student, the teacher responds that there was no point in trying to get that student to participate because he was going to fail no matter what. The teacher's response demonstrates a disagreement with which educational philosophy?

a. Teach students to be life-long learners.
b. Education is the key to success.
c. All students can learn.
d. Educate the whole child.

31. Which of the following best represents a threat to a physically safe campus environment?

a. Inefficient arrival and dismissal procedures
b. High student-to-teacher classroom ratios
c. High teacher turnover
d. Electrical hazards

32. Which of the following is the most critical question to consider when using community resources in the classroom?

a. Are the resources aligned with the curriculum?
b. Are there enough resources for all students?
c. Are teachers familiar with these resources?
d. Are the resources expected to be returned?

33. Which of the following actions best demonstrates collaboration with teachers to maintain an instructional program that delivers standards-based instruction?

a. Audit instructional materials used in the classroom, including worksheets and teacher-developed materials.
b. Compare student course grades to performance on standardized tests.
c. Engage in professional learning communities with teachers to contribute to planning discussions about the curriculum.
d. Survey teachers to obtain feedback about new curriculum options.

Copyright © Mometrix Media. You have been licensed one copy of this document for personal use only. Any other reproduction or redistribution is strictly prohibited. All rights reserved.
This content is provided for test preparation purposes only and does not imply an endorsement by Mometrix of any particular political, scientific, or religious point of view.

34. The majority of US state laws designate which school professionals as mandated reporters of child abuse and neglect?

a. Healthcare and mental health professionals, but not childcare providers
b. Teachers, principals, and other school personnel are required to report
c. Social workers instead of school social workers are mandated reporters
d. Law enforcement officers, but not medical examiners and coroners

35. A school leader is developing a plan for effective use of an annex building on the school property. Which of the following staff members would be able to best assist the school leader in developing this plan?

a. A lead teacher
b. The plant operator
c. An assistant principal
d. The district superintendent

36. Which of the following actions best illustrates how a school leader engages with the community in a proactive manner?

a. The school leader attends all local school board meetings.
b. The school leader attends the community holiday parade.
c. The school leader hosts an award ceremony for students at the school.
d. The school leader purchases advertisement space in the local community newspaper.

37. What have researchers found regarding the relationship between student academic self-concepts and student outcomes?

a. Students' academic self-concepts are correlated with success later in life.
b. Students' academic self-concepts are correlated with their academic achievement.
c. Students' academic self-concepts are correlated with socioeconomic status more than home settings.
d. Students' academic self-concepts are correlated with enrollment in smaller schools.

38. Of the following, which accurately reflects a principle of adult learning that applies to professional development (PD) for teachers?

a. Adults learn best when participation in PD is required.
b. Adults learn best when learning materials are selected and provided.
c. Adults learn best when they are involved in planning the instruction.
d. Adults learn best when informed about how they will be assessed prior to participation.

39. Which of the following should school principals primarily look for when observing teachers in classrooms for evaluation purposes?

a. They should focus on what students want to learn rather than what they want them to learn.
b. They should look for how comfortable the teacher is with the lesson content and method of delivery.
c. They should look for evidence of learning such as student responses to checks for understanding and student work products.
d. They should focus on physical classroom setup.

Copyright © Mometrix Media. You have been licensed one copy of this document for personal use only. Any other reproduction or redistribution is strictly prohibited. All rights reserved.
This content is provided for test preparation purposes only and does not imply an endorsement by Mometrix of any particular political, scientific, or religious point of view.

40. A school leader conducts a needs assessment for the school using student academic performance data, student attendance data, student focus groups, and teacher focus groups. The leader then decides to conduct an anonymous survey of community stakeholders. The primary benefit of this action is that:

a. The leader will increase buy in from the community.
b. Surveying the community will increase community engagement.
c. The school leader will be able to explain past school performance.
d. The school leader will have multiple sources of data to conduct a thorough needs assessment.

41. Which of the following accurately represents how school leaders can promote equitable access to curriculum for all students and their parents?

a. They can make staff more comfortable in discussing diversity without promoting equity.
b. They can clarify school staff misconceptions related to deficit theories about minorities.
c. They can model equity in daily interactions, but should avoid confronting discrimination.
d. They can create safe environments, though student support networks are not their job.

42. Which of the following principles about formative assessment should school leaders consider when giving feedback to and collaborating with teachers?

a. Student motivation and learning are unaffected by assessment types.
b. Student motivation and learning are affected by assessment types.
c. Error is inevitable in all assessment, and only summative assessment is a valid indicator of student learning.
d. Student performance against a standard is more important than student growth.

43. Which of the following is most effective in motivating members of the educational community when implementing new policies?

a. Delegating authority to staff members
b. Communicating unexpected barriers to the community as they arise
c. Sharing the policies frequently using a variety of communication channels
d. Including stakeholders in the development of new policies

44. Several teachers on campus have expressed concerns to the principal that there is too much focus on standardized assessment. The teachers suggest that they develop authentic assessments for student learning. Which of the following is the best example of authentic summative assessment?

a. Benchmark tests
b. Student choice of completing a project, essay, or performance
c. Oral exams
d. Allowing students to complete homework assignments at their own pace

45. According to experts, applying systems thinking to school organizations results in which of these characteristics?

a. Policies and practices of school systems are improved continuously.
b. Curricula become diversified within the school system.
c. School systems become independent of other community systems.
d. Priorities are identified for the success of targeted student groups.

Copyright © Mometrix Media. You have been licensed one copy of this document for personal use only. Any other reproduction or redistribution is strictly prohibited. All rights reserved.
This content is provided for test preparation purposes only and does not imply an endorsement by Mometrix of any particular political, scientific, or religious point of view.

46. Which of the following would be most likely to cause an administrator to look for outside resources in assisting students and their families?

a. A student is having difficulty in math class.
b. Two students participated in a physical altercation.
c. A student and his or her family are struggling financially and are in need of food and clothing.
d. A student will be the first in the family to graduate high school.

47. What do psychologists recommend regarding tiered models of student behavior management in education?

a. Tiered models of behavior management work only with school-wide behavior support systems.
b. Tiered models of behavior management are most effective when addressing individual disruptive student behavior.
c. Tiered models of behavior management are most applicable for classroom or school-wide implementation.
d. Tiered models of behavior management are judged best for individuals, classrooms, or schools.

48. In reference to the Supportive School Discipline Initiative (SSDI), former US Attorney General Eric Holder said a federal initiative to guide school disciplinary practices would "make schools safe, supportive and inclusive for all students" and would "keep America's young people safe and on the right path." How did he say it would do these things?

a. By making discipline less exclusionary
b. By divorcing discipline from civil rights
c. By getting data from resource officers
d. By referring discipline to peace officers

49. A school leader is developing a process for continuous improvement on campus. Which of the following actions should the school leader take first?

a. Develop evaluation procedures and set checkpoints for evaluation.
b. Train staff on the continuous improvement process.
c. Select a low performing area that needs to be addressed.
d. Identify strategies for addressing low performing areas.

50. Which of the following represents an effective step that a school leader can take to change negative assumptions about teaching diverse populations?

a. Conduct diversity training with all staff.
b. Create a mentoring program on campus.
c. Publish an official statement on diversity and inclusion.
d. Only hire teachers that represent the student demographics.

51. Which of these is a valid guideline for school leaders to support staff throughout their professional development (PD)?

a. To be job-embedded and school-based, PD must occur in the school building.
b. For effective PD, teachers must not learn passively, but be actively involved.
c. Because teachers are the ones involved in PD, it should be teacher-centered.
d. PD must be done independently to ensure individual learning and growth.

Copyright © Mometrix Media. You have been licensed one copy of this document for personal use only. Any other reproduction or redistribution is strictly prohibited. All rights reserved.
This content is provided for test preparation purposes only and does not imply an endorsement by Mometrix of any particular political, scientific, or religious point of view.

52. When schools and leaders implement the continuous school improvement process, which should they do *first*?

a. Establish specific goals for school improvements
b. Reflect on instructional and leadership practices
c. Implement strategies for specific improvements
d. Conduct needs assessments for their schools

53. Which of the following is the best way that a school leader can ensure equitable treatment of students and staff?

a. Develop policies and procedures and adhere to them.
b. Create advisory committees with representatives from a variety of diverse demographics.
c. Create a diversity and inclusion statement for the school.
d. Address student and staff complaints swiftly.

54. Which of the following best represents a mutually beneficial relationship between a school and a community organization?

a. A neighborhood grocery store donates bottled water to the basketball team for home games.
b. The school hosts a clothing drive for a local homeless shelter once a year.
c. A local church has permission to use the school library for meetings on Saturday mornings and the principal is permitted to make announcements to the attendees during the meetings.
d. A medical clinic near the school offers free immunizations and physicals to students actively enrolled at the school.

55. Alternative high school principals Mohr and Dichter (2001) codified developmental stages that school staff undergo to become learning communities. Which stage is associated with the emergence of a sense of community?

a. The stage involving conflict
b. The honeymoon stage
c. The confusion stage
d. The mature stage

56. When school leaders and school district personnel plan school budgets according to budget allocations issued by their school district, which of the following is correct?

a. It is most difficult to project employee salaries for the next school year.
b. Employee benefits are more difficult to predict than employee salaries.
c. Transportation expenses are included in budgets as these are essential.
d. School districts cannot reserve funds for unplanned emergency repairs.

57. Which of the following factors may directly affect a school leader's ability to recruit and retain highly qualified teachers?

a. The number of recruitment fairs that a school leader attends
b. The percentage of experienced teachers already on campus
c. The school culture
d. The available technology on campus

Copyright © Mometrix Media. You have been licensed one copy of this document for personal use only. Any other reproduction or redistribution is strictly prohibited. All rights reserved.
This content is provided for test preparation purposes only and does not imply an endorsement by Mometrix of any particular political, scientific, or religious point of view.

58. A group of community members meet with the principal to share concerns that the community does not believe the principal is effectively communicating data about progress toward the school vision and goals. The community members explain that many of them are not able to attend meetings held at the school. Which of the following solutions should the principal suggest to the community members?

a. Change the dates and times that community meetings are held so that more people can attend.
b. Have community members who attend the meetings inform others who did not attend about what was discussed at the meeting.
c. Refer community members to the school website where the meeting minutes are posted.
d. Develop a variety of ways to communicate in addition to the community meetings, such as via email, a school newsletter, and regular phone calls.

59. Which of the following practices by school leaders most effectively improves teacher practice and student learning?

a. Reviewing student performance data and sharing aggregated results with teachers
b. Administering self-assessment surveys to teachers
c. Conducting regular classroom observations and providing timely feedback
d. Offering educational resources to teachers related to their identified areas of weakness

60. Which of the following is indicative of a school that is focused on encouraging intercultural awareness in students?

a. Social studies classrooms are required to include one research project per year that focuses on different cultures.
b. The principal invites African American guest speakers to the campus for Black History Month.
c. The principal publishes a statement about diversity and inclusion on the school website.
d. The principal adds American Sign Language to the foreign language course offerings.

61. Which of the following is the best way to identify strategies for facilitating change?

a. Host student and teacher focus groups to solicit suggestions and ideas.
b. Conduct pilot programs and collect data to determine efficacy.
c. Study research-based and proven best practices.
d. Meet with community stakeholders to solicit suggestions and ideas.

62. Which of the following best represents a threat to an emotionally safe campus environment?

a. Bullying
b. Crowded classrooms
c. High teacher turnover
d. High rates of student suspensions

63. Regarding acceptable use policies (AUPs) for student Internet access in public schools, which statement is most applicable?

a. The most important factor is the fundamental right of Americans to information access.
b. School district AUPs always require student agreement and parental permission forms.
c. A workable school AUP should achieve a balance between freedom and responsibility.
d. Schools should not consult outside organizations about digital freedom of information.

Copyright © Mometrix Media. You have been licensed one copy of this document for personal use only. Any other reproduction or redistribution is strictly prohibited. All rights reserved.
This content is provided for test preparation purposes only and does not imply an endorsement by Mometrix of any particular political, scientific, or religious point of view.

64. Which of the following professional development activities would likely have the most impact on current teacher performance?

a. A self-paced book study program for all teachers
b. Online courses that teachers select and participate in at their own pace.
c. A four-hour in-person training conducted during the school year
d. A hybrid online and in-person six-week course that meets weekly for a cohort of teachers

65. What should school leaders keep in mind when integrating technology into standards-based curricula?

a. They should assign their teachers to write technology standards.
b. They cannot help students meet standards by using technology.
c. They do not need to require students to master technology standards.
d. They should focus on learning with technology, not learning about it.

66. Which of the following best illustrates the connection between the school community and local employment trends?

a. A school begins to offer health care courses and training in response to a need for more healthcare workers in the community.
b. The school librarian partners with the neighborhood library to share resources.
c. A school sets a goal to increase the graduation rate.
d. A school increases the number of dual-credit college courses offered on campus.

67. Which of the following is the best example of summative assessment?

a. Standardized tests
b. Homework assignments
c. Practice assignments completed in class
d. Projects

68. A dean of instruction of a middle school wants to increase the number and variety of resources that teachers have access to. Which of the following actions should the dean take to accomplish this goal?

a. Encourage teachers to purchase instructional resources and provide reimbursement for their expenses.
b. Survey teachers to identify which resources they would like to have and purchase resources from their suggestions.
c. Provide teachers with asynchronous, on-demand professional development sessions online.
d. Seek free and discounted resources from vendors in the local area.

69. Which of the following is most used in self-assessment to facilitate professional development?

a. Teachers write in journals about their work
b. Teachers apply advice they receive to work
c. Teachers analyze videos of their instruction
d. Teachers benefit from others' experiences

Copyright © Mometrix Media. You have been licensed one copy of this document for personal use only. Any other reproduction or redistribution is strictly prohibited. All rights reserved.
This content is provided for test preparation purposes only and does not imply an endorsement by Mometrix of any particular political, scientific, or religious point of view.

70. A high school principal determines that it is no longer financially viable to sponsor the fine arts program at the school. Enrollment in fine arts courses has steadily decreased over the past four school years and the expenses of the program have exceeded the budget. However, the principal knows that many stakeholders in the community feel strongly about having a fine arts program. Which of the following represents the best action for the school principal?

a. Continue to offer the fine arts program.
b. Make an announcement to the students and staff that there will not be a fine arts program next year.
c. Host a fundraiser for the fine arts program.
d. Host a meeting to explain to stakeholders the reasons for eliminating the fine arts program.

Constructed Response

1. You are starting your first year as principal at Mendoza High School, which has a diverse student population of about 1,500 students. Over the past several years the pass rate on the state mandated English exam has been declining and is now notably lower than the pass rate in other area high schools. Last school year (prior to your beginning at the school) the English department in conjunction with the faculty audited the school's curriculum and adjusted it to align with the state standards. This year, the superintendent has told you that you will have an additional $12,000 in discretionary funds to support the initiative to increase the pass rate of the English exam. In 300-600 words, outline two important issues you should consider when preparing recommendations for the discretionary budget, explain one strategy you can use to determine budget allocations to recommend that will promote improved student performance, and explain why the strategy you have described will likely be effective.

2. You are the principal of a 900-student middle school (6-8). The school recently formulated a school vision, which includes a critical goal of improving the academic and social-emotional preparedness of the school's eighth-graders for the transition to high school. Over the past several years, teachers and administrators in the local high school have become increasingly concerned about the level of preparedness of incoming ninth-grade students, who have been increasingly socially immature and lacking in vital academic and study skills. Various stakeholders (parents, students, teachers in both schools) attribute the problem to different reasons and would prescribe different remedies. You form a committee to improve the transition to high school for the eighth-graders in your school. Committee members include teachers, parents, student supports (social worker, school psychologist), a special education representative, and a curriculum coordinator.

Write a 150-300 word memo to the members of the committee about the plan to improve eighth-grade readiness for high school. Before you write the memo, state what assumptions you make about the school/community (rural/urban, demographics, socioeconomics). In the memo convey why you believe it is important for the school to succeed in this endeavor (improving preparedness for high school) and describe 2-3 significant aspects of the school's instructional program that the committee will address in developing its plan. For each of these specific aspects/factors describe a type of data or other information that the team should analyze and explain why this type of information may be useful in analyzing the specific area of concern.

Copyright © Mometrix Media. You have been licensed one copy of this document for personal use only. Any other reproduction or redistribution is strictly prohibited. All rights reserved.
This content is provided for test preparation purposes only and does not imply an endorsement by Mometrix of any particular political, scientific, or religious point of view.

Answer Key and Explanations for Test #1

Multiple Choice Questions

1. A: Leaders intent on fostering change are required to strategically communicate the intended change and gather supporters for that change. First, the leader needs to communicate the intended change effectively. Many people are unwilling to support changes because they fear the unknown. The leader should communicate not only what is to be changed but also how the changes affect the various staff members and how the changes are aligned to the school vision and goals.

2. C: Staff growth though professional development is important. When identifying professional development for staff members, school leaders should consider school goals as well as individual goals of staff members. This will ensure that staff members are equipped to contribute to achieving school goals but also grow in areas that they have established personal goals.

3. C: Shared leadership, regular monitoring of progress, and accountability of everyone participating in implementation are key elements to consistent goal implementation. Sharing leadership creates buy in for the vision and empowers others to take action so that the leader is not solely responsible for making progress toward the vision. Regular monitoring of goal progress using milestones and timelines keeps everyone on pace for implementing the goals and vision. The leader must also hold people accountable because each person must do their part in order for the plan to be implemented successfully and according to schedule.

4. D: The ultimate responsibility of developing and implementing professional development for teachers and staff belongs to the school leader. However, a school leader should leverage the knowledge and expertise of the administrative team and teacher leaders in this process. The school leader may provide the overall vision and goals and delegate some of the responsibilities relating to professional development to others while holding all parties accountable for meeting goals and aligning to the vision.

5. D: School system guidelines recommend that, in giving teachers observational feedback, school leaders should focus feedback discussions by developing open-ended questions that target specific areas for each teacher, explicitly name two or three teacher strengths they observed, identify one area for improvement that will make the most impact on student learning and teacher development, and develop a few specific and attainable next steps for each teacher to take. Effective observational feedback should include strengths and weaknesses and recommendations for next steps should be clear and attainable.

6. C: The school leader observing classroom instruction can also observe students in the learning process. Classroom observations can provide valuable information about instructional delivery, teacher quality, and student performance. Reviewing classroom observation data in conjunction with student academic performance data can provide the school leader with a more well-rounded understanding of the quality of learning on campus.

7. D: School leaders must maintain rigorous standards-based instruction across the campus. If students are not able to meet the standards, additional supports and interventions must be offered to students to address educational gaps. The math teacher cannot choose to lower the expectations or standards for students without permission and documentation according to local and state policies. The teacher does not demonstrate a need for training related to implementation of the curriculum, but the teacher must be directed to abide by the curriculum as written.

Copyright © Mometrix Media. You have been licensed one copy of this document for personal use only. Any other reproduction or redistribution is strictly prohibited. All rights reserved.
This content is provided for test preparation purposes only and does not imply an endorsement by Mometrix of any particular political, scientific, or religious point of view.

8. A: Research studies have found the most effective implementations of school data use initiatives were most proactive, offering regular and expert system data use training of school leaders, leadership skills advice and coaching, and vigorous promotion. These got significantly better results even comparing districts using similar data systems, showing implementation was more important than the data system. Researchers observed that, although technology is necessary to support data initiatives, it alone is not the answer to school data use. Studies also found teams use data technology systems more quickly and productively than individual teachers.

9. D: Because research studies repeatedly prove student benefits of smaller class sizes, school leaders must hire and retain adequate human resources in terms of quantity and quality. For a safe, comfortable teaching and learning environment, school leaders must provide adequate physical resources like space, furniture, lighting, temperature control, etc. They must manage fiscal resources well to manage all other resources, not just some.

10. A: Each of the suggestions are viable options for the school leader to implement; however, the school leader needs to know why teachers leave or plan to leave in order to best address the problem. Seeking feedback from the teaching staff can help the school leader to focus resources on the most direct causes of teacher attrition. Once the causes are identified, the school leader can determine if the other suggestions are applicable.

11. A: The Individuals with Disabilities Education Act (IDEA) and Family Rights and Privacy Act (FERPA) both define the same document types as educational records (B). FERPA determines conditions for educational records destruction based on state laws (C). IDEA amendments regarding educational records collection, maintenance, confidentiality, disclosure (D), and destruction (C) are based on FERPA. However, the IDEA requires designating special education records custodians to ensure the instruction and training of all educators collecting confidential information, but FERPA does not (A).

12. C: To realize their school goals for students despite economic constraints, instead of the common but counterproductive school reactions of postponing improvements or cutting services and programs students need, school leaders can identify programs that are expensive but do not improve student performance while considering different alternatives for achieving the same results, like providing professional development less expensively by implementing study groups instead of paying for guest speakers and workshops.

13. C: A successful new teacher induction program will provide opportunities for new teachers to collaborate with one another and with more experienced teachers. Additionally, a successful program will incorporate leadership development opportunities for new teachers to explore and refine their leadership skills. New teachers should receive strategic professional coaching and be assigned a mentor based on experience and effectiveness of the mentoring staff member. While the school leader is responsible for ensuring that an effective induction program in place, there are other instructional staff and campus leaders who can add value to the induction program by facilitating various aspects of the program.

14. B: Creating an advisory committee and meeting with the committee regularly demonstrates that the leader is willing to hear other perspectives and opinions prior to making decisions. A school leader may believe one course of action is correct but then change their mind after receiving feedback from an advisory committee. A school leader can demonstrate a willingness to change by getting information from a variety of sources prior to making decisions.

Copyright © Mometrix Media. You have been licensed one copy of this document for personal use only. Any other reproduction or redistribution is strictly prohibited. All rights reserved.
This content is provided for test preparation purposes only and does not imply an endorsement by Mometrix of any particular political, scientific, or religious point of view.

15. A: A school must hold a Manifestation Determination Review within 10 school days according to the following criteria: if the school is seeking to change student placement for more than 10 consecutive days for disciplinary reasons; if the school suspends a student for disciplinary reasons for more than 10 cumulative days that form a pattern; the school is deciding to expel or otherwise exclude a student for disciplinary reasons; or the school convenes this meeting after a disciplinary incident.

16. A: A school leader must create structures in the school programming that promote collaboration for teachers. Allotting time in the master schedule for co-planning ensures that teachers will have dedicated time to collaborate, such as by participating in professional learning communities. Offering to pay teachers to stay after school may not be effective because some teachers may opt-out. Additionally, these planning sessions could interfere with other school activities these teachers may be involved in, such as coaching or tutoring. Providing asynchronous collaboration online could potentially be helpful, but it is not the best choice since it likely will not lead to real-time collaboration. Removing qualified teachers for planning can negatively impact student performance and should be used sparingly, if at all.

17. A: A supportive school climate occurs when students have resources readily available to them that can help them feel supported and to overcome challenges that they may face. The resources available should be based on student needs, such as counseling, mentorship, social activities, and others. A supportive school climate should foster peer relationships among peers intentionally rather than allowing them to happen by chance because students share common schedules. While policy handbooks for students are useful, they do not directly contribute to a supportive school environment. On the other hand, student interactions with adults on campus can directly impact students' feelings of being supported.

18. A: When a school leader has clearly and effectively communicated the school vision and goals, others will be able to describe them in their own words. They will be able to communicate the vision and goals to others and explain the rationale behind them. Stakeholders who understand the vision and goals will propose ideas and actions that are aligned to the vision and will understand how they can participate in or contribute to achieving the vision.

19. C: Most school expenditures are related to classroom instruction. These expenditures include teacher salaries, libraries, professional development for teachers, curriculum development, and instructional technology. Operations is the next highest percentage of budgetary expenditures, followed by administration and student support services. Student support services involve expenses such as social work, guidance, health expenses, and psychological services.

20. B: Testing accommodations for some students based on their individual needs are not unfair, but actually make assessments fairer and also more valid. School leaders can help decrease achievement gaps among student cultural groups and backgrounds by using student data to monitor progress regularly. However, extensive testing of students, especially to the impediment of instruction, can be detrimental to students who are already low performing. Data collected from assessments, even non-standardized formative assessments, can be used to monitor student progress and inform instructional decisions.

21. B: FERPA stands for the Family Educational Rights and Privacy Act. It is a federal law that protects student information and education records.

22. B: The disproportionate number of students suspended from school based on race may indicate that there are beliefs influencing how teachers relate to students. The school principal needs to

Copyright © Mometrix Media. You have been licensed one copy of this document for personal use only. Any other reproduction or redistribution is strictly prohibited. All rights reserved.
This content is provided for test preparation purposes only and does not imply an endorsement by Mometrix of any particular political, scientific, or religious point of view.

identify if there is evidence of this in the school culture and whether campus policies perpetuate negative beliefs.

23. C: The school board elects or hires and supervises the superintendent, who in turns hires and supervises the school principal. In the hierarchy of public education leadership, the school board makes policy decisions based on state and local legislature and the superintendent implements these policies. School principals apply these policies to the daily operations of the school. There may be instances in which a principal participates in a school board meeting, such as by reporting data or speaking, but these activities are not part of the regular responsibilities of a principal in relation to the school board.

24. B: The goal is for both teachers and students to improve their computer skills; providing training to teachers or a new course for students does not fully address the school goal. Purchasing updated computers for students and teachers and training them to use the devices best demonstrates that the leader is using school resources to support the school goal.

25. C: Meeting with a diverse group of stakeholders from the community will give the new principal a well-rounded perspective of the community. Researching the community online, reviewing student data, and talking with staff are all effective methods of collecting information, but speaking directly with community members is a better source of more insightful information.

26. D: Although each of these options could negatively impact the math performance goal, the loss of a math teacher directly impacts student learning and performance. Student performance in math is directly related to the quality of instruction that students receive in the classroom, meaning that the absence of a qualified math teacher for any length of time can be impactful. Additionally, the unexpected loss of a teacher can be a difficult obstacle to address in a timely manner. It is likely that losing a math teacher would negatively impact the goal.

27. A: Prior to adopting curriculum, the alignment of the curriculum to learning standards must be verified. Curriculum that is not aligned will not be effective in instruction students and ensuring their performance on state-mandated assessments. After the alignment has been verified, the curriculum may be vetted by various stakeholders and approved for use by the school board.

28. B: Community resources can be used in a variety of ways, such as providing school supplies for students, facilitating field trips, and providing mentorship. However, providing tutorial services to students most directly supports student learning. Tutoring students directly impacts student academic performance in class, whereas the other community resources support students' economic and psychosocial needs that may only impact learning indirectly.

29. C: The use of school funds represents a common ethical situation. All school funds should be used according to policies and procedures outlined by the school board. Using school funds for personal use is a violation of ethics.

30. C: When a person finds value and worth in each student, they exemplify the educational philosophy that all students can learn. Some students may need more support or different resources, but they still have the capacity to learn. This teacher's statement that the student would fail anyway is in direct opposition to this philosophy.

31. D: A physically safe environment is free from dangers, both seen and unseen, that would pose a threat to the physical safety of anyone exposed to the environment. A physically safe environment is in good repair, accessible to all, and accommodating in relation to the nature in which the environment is designated for use.

Copyright © Mometrix Media. You have been licensed one copy of this document for personal use only. Any other reproduction or redistribution is strictly prohibited. All rights reserved.
This content is provided for test preparation purposes only and does not imply an endorsement by Mometrix of any particular political, scientific, or religious point of view.

32. A: Community resources used in the school must align with school programming. As a result, resources that will be used in the classroom must align with the curriculum. While it is important to consider a variety of other factors prior to incorporating community resources into the curriculum, it is imperative that the resources are aligned with the school vision and goals, which include the curriculum.

33. C: Collaboration requires that the school leader engage directly with teachers to maintain an instructional program that delivers standards-based instruction. PLCs are excellent opportunities to listen and provide input during the planning stage for delivering instruction. Auditing classroom materials and analyzing the accuracy of grading are good tools for evaluating the delivery of standards-based instruction but are not collaborative. Administering a survey about new curriculum is not collaborative and does not help to support implementation of current materials.

34. B: As of 2013, New Jersey and Wyoming required *all* persons to report child abuse and neglect; all other US states identified specific professionals as mandated reporters. These professions include healthcare and mental health professionals *and* childcare providers; teachers, principals, and other school personnel; social workers, *including* school social workers; law enforcement officers; and medical examiners or coroners.

35. B: The plant operator oversees the operation of the school campus from a facilities standpoint. This staff member will have information related to the physical layout of the facility, its intended use, accessibility, and many other aspects of the physical building that will be helpful in determining how the building can be used appropriately.

36. B: Participating in school- and district-sponsored events is not always the same as engaging with the greater community. Community stakeholders can include members of the community who do not have children enrolled in the school district but are contributors to the community as a whole. These stakeholders may include business owners, community organization leaders, and residents near the school. Additionally, community engagement involves opportunities for two-way communication between the school leader and community members. Attending the community parade gives the school leader an opportunity to represent the school at a community event and engage with community stakeholders. This increases the school leader's visibility in the community and demonstrates that the school is a part of the community that it serves.

37. A: Researchers have found that students' academic self-concepts are *not correlated* with their academic achievement, but *are* correlated with later life successes like employment and earnings. Although socioeconomic status (SES) is related to academic self-concept (as well as achievement and retention), it does *not* correlate as strongly with SES as with students' home educational settings. Although smaller school size is found to benefit student participation as well as principal leadership and teacher distributed leadership, *larger* school size correlates positively with student academic self-concept.

38. C: Adults learn in more productive ways when the choice to learn is voluntary, when they have choices among learning materials, when they are involved in planning the instruction they will be accessing, and when they are able to give instructors input about how their learning will be assessed.

39. C: School principals should look for evidence of learning when conducting a classroom observation. Students should be given opportunities to respond and demonstrate learning throughout the lesson so that the teacher and the observer can determine whether students are learning the content. These opportunities may occur as questioning strategies, discussion, or

Copyright © Mometrix Media. You have been licensed one copy of this document for personal use only. Any other reproduction or redistribution is strictly prohibited. All rights reserved.
This content is provided for test preparation purposes only and does not imply an endorsement by Mometrix of any particular political, scientific, or religious point of view.

through guided and independent practice. It is important for teachers to be comfortable with the instructional content and method of delivery, but this is not a primary focus of a classroom observation as a novice teacher can be nervous yet still effective. Additionally, the physical classroom setup should be conducive to learning but is not the primary focus of a classroom observation.

40. D: All the choices are benefits of gathering the data, but the primary benefit is obtaining multiple sources of data to accurately identify the strengths, needs, gaps, and areas of improvement for the school. The school leader chose a combination of quantitative and qualitative data to accurately assess school performance and the cultures, values, attitudes, and beliefs that impact that performance. It is important to use data from multiple sources to develop the school vision and goals because using only one source of data may portray a limited or skewed picture of the school. Using multiple sources of data can confirm the validity of data and provide a more complete picture of the complex dynamics of a school campus.

41. B: School leaders can promote equitable access to curriculum for all students and parents by making staff more comfortable discussing diversity issues, social justice, and values, which will promote equity; clarifying staff misconceptions related to deficit theories about minorities and diverse groups; modeling equity beliefs and behaviors in daily interactions; confronting discrimination and stereotyping in actions and language; creating safe school environments where all students feel welcomed and valued; and establishing support networks for students harassed over cultural, sexual, and/or gender identity.

42. B: To provide teachers with effective feedback and collaboration, school leaders must know that student motivation and learning are influenced by different types of assessments; that despite "objective" tests, machine scoring, etc., ultimately assessment is based in the judgment, assumptions, and values of professional educators who design, score, interpret, and grade assessments; that not only is error inevitable in all assessment, but moreover it is typically underestimated; and that reliability in assessment involves scores and results, *not* tests or instruments.

43. D: New policies should be well communicated in vision and in methodology, but if the policy comes directly from the leadership without having shared motivation the community as a whole will not have buy in and the implementation is likely to face resistance. Delegating authority to staff is a great way of involving stakeholders within the school building but does not include members of the school community who are not employed at the school. Communicating frequently is effective for sharing the vision but does not necessarily motivate community members to participate in implementing new ideas, policies, and procedures.

44. B: Traditional methods of assessment usually involve a standardized test with closed questions that require students to select an answer from several choices. Authentic assessment allows students to demonstrate mastery of content and objectives in different ways within the context of the subject matter. This may include project assessments, writing assessments, and performance assessment. The goal of authentic assessment is to provide students with the opportunity to authentically demonstrate that they have mastered the content.

45. A: According to the American Association of School Administrators (AASA) Center for System Leadership, applying systems thinking to school reform results in, among other things, continuous improvement of school system policies and practices. Curriculum is aligned system-wide, not diversified. The school system grows in interconnection with other community systems and does

Copyright © Mometrix Media. You have been licensed one copy of this document for personal use only. Any other reproduction or redistribution is strictly prohibited. All rights reserved.
This content is provided for test preparation purposes only and does not imply an endorsement by Mometrix of any particular political, scientific, or religious point of view.

not become independent. Priorities are identified and resources are allocated accordingly for universal student success, not only targeted student groups.

46. C: Depending on school budget and resources, student needs that are not directly related to student safety and academic performance may not be able to be addressed using school resources. Many community resources used to support schools are targeted toward students in need. These types of resources may address physical needs of students and their families, such as providing food, clothing, toiletries, haircuts and grooming, or helping adults find jobs.

47. D: The American Psychological Association (APA) recommends a tiered model of behavior management above all others for schools—i.e., a system of positive behavior supports that includes both prevention and intervention with primary, secondary, and tertiary levels—not only for school-wide systems or only for disruptive behaviors of individual students, but for both of these as well as for classroom behavior management.

48. A: The Supportive School Discipline Initiative (SSDI) included guidance for positive school discipline practices to keep students in school by providing alternatives to exclusionary methods like suspension and expulsion. This guidance was produced jointly by the US Departments of Education and Justice to ensure enforcement of federal civil rights protections against discrimination. It provides school resources with helpful information rather than getting it from them. The SSDI's purpose was to keep student discipline from escalating to the police or prison systems, not to continue this trend.

49. A: The process of continuous improvement is the ongoing act of assessing performance and adjusting efforts in order to improve that performance. In order to implement a process of continuous improvement, there must be procedures of evaluation developed and implemented at regular checkpoints. Based on these regular evaluations, the leadership team can identify areas of improvement and initiate interventions and actions based on those identified areas. In schools, the regular evaluation of progress toward the campus vision and goals can be developed into a process of continuous improvement. However, campus leaders must focus on both the strengths and weaknesses of the campus in this process. Deficient areas can be improved to perform to standard, while areas performing at standard can be innovated for improvement.

50. A: All staff can benefit from diversity training so they can challenge any negative assumptions that they may have about various populations of students or staff. School leaders must take caution not to allow negative assumptions and beliefs to impact the hiring process or the implementation of policies and procedures on campus.

51. B: Although professional development (PD) must be job-embedded and school-based, it can occur even outside of the school building if teachers view it as part of their daily work duties and it emerges from and contributes to daily classroom practice. Teachers must be actively involved in the learning process for effective PD. It should be student-centered so that teachers learn to support student learning because PD is not for teachers' own sake. Collaborative teacher problem-solving is a PD guideline because it is valuable, addresses the issue of teacher isolation, and fosters professional and community respect.

52. D: In a cycle of continuous school improvement driven by data that they collect and analyze, schools and leaders should first conduct a needs assessment for their school to identify where to focus improvement efforts. Once they have identified needs, they should set specific improvement goals. Then they should reflect on their teaching and leading practices for further informing

Copyright © Mometrix Media. You have been licensed one copy of this document for personal use only. Any other reproduction or redistribution is strictly prohibited. All rights reserved.
This content is provided for test preparation purposes only and does not imply an endorsement by Mometrix of any particular political, scientific, or religious point of view.

improvement. This enables implementing improvement strategies. Another necessary step is to assess progress during and following implementation.

53. A: The best way that the school leader can ensure equitable treatment of students and staff is to develop policies and procedures and adhere to them. When there are policies and procedures in place, the school leader can refer to these to determine their course of action when dealing with students and staff. Policies and procedures help leaders proactively ensure that students and staff are treated equitably because they serve as guidelines for behavior and are not subjective. Creating an advisory committee can assist with developing these policies and procedures, but doing so does not shape the behavior of all staff and students. Additionally, while it is advisable that a school leader addresses student and staff complaints swiftly, this is a reactive response and likely occurs after someone has already been treated in an inequitable manner.

54. C: This scenario best represents a mutually beneficial relationship. The church has the benefit of having a meeting place and the principal has the benefit of communicating directly with community members on a regular basis. The other activities help to build positive relationships between the school and the community, but are one-sided.

55. B: Alternative high school principals (Mohr and Dichter, 2001) identified staff developmental stages of honeymoon, conflict, confusion, messy, scary, and mature, in that order, in becoming learning communities. The honeymoon stage is identified as when a sense of community first emerges. The conflict stage is summarized as "the honeymoon is over." The confusion stage is characterized by staff uncertainty over the leader's role. The messy stage involves increased lack of clarity. The scary stage finds staff wondering where accountability and authority are. The mature stage equates to the birth of a learning community.

56. B: School leaders and district personnel can usually project employee salaries for the next school year fairly easily, but it is more difficult to predict healthcare or other employee benefits. Although transportation expenses are essential, they are *not* included in school budgets. Not only are regular school buses and drivers expensive, individual transportation plans included in special education students' Individualized Education Program (IEPs) are even more so, and furnishing homeless and/or other students with transportation is yet another expense. In addition, school district planners *must* reserve some amount of the budget for unexpected emergency school facility repairs, etc.

57. C: The school culture can create a welcoming environment for new teachers, or it can repel them. When the school culture is positive, focused on students, and driven by excellence, teachers will want to be a part of that culture. They will be motivated by the positive culture and will recruit others to join the team. On the other hand, if the school culture is negative, then teachers and staff will likely have negative attitudes as well. Teachers will seek a way out of that school environment rather than encouraging others to join the team. This negative culture can negatively affect students' academic performance and behavior. If a potential teacher candidate observes a negative school culture, they may be unwilling to work at that campus.

58. D: A leader should frequently communicate with parents and the community about progress toward goals in a variety of ways. This can include community meetings, but communication should not be limited to in-person meetings. The leader can provide a newsletter or bulletin that will update the community about school performance, upcoming events, and ways to get involved with the school to help achieve the school goals. Many schools feature phone systems that can mass call students' homes, which can be used to communicate announcements regarding school goals and

Copyright © Mometrix Media. You have been licensed one copy of this document for personal use only. Any other reproduction or redistribution is strictly prohibited. All rights reserved.
This content is provided for test preparation purposes only and does not imply an endorsement by Mometrix of any particular political, scientific, or religious point of view.

progress toward those goals. Similarly, school leaders can mail letters to parents containing updates regarding the school goals.

59. C: Providing ongoing feedback to teachers has the most significant impact on teacher performance. School leaders are responsible for evaluating teachers, providing feedback on evaluations, and assisting teachers with improving areas of weakness through coaching, mentoring, professional development, and other strategies.

60. A: This action best represents an effort to develop a culture of knowledge about and comfort with cultures other than the students' own. Whereas knowledge doesn't always have highly noticeable effects on the school culture in the short-term, it has long-term impact on the community because it helps to break down ignorance about other cultures. Students who know something about another culture are much more willing to interact with people from that culture, rather than avoid peers who are not like themselves. This is particularly helpful when implemented as a schoolwide policy rather than occurring in individual classes because it will have a greater impact on the entire culture of the school. Black History Month should be celebrated, but it only provides perspectives from one culture and doesn't necessarily encourage interaction between various cultures. Publishing a statement about diversity and inclusion likely does not show a strong enough gesture to encourage real change. Adding ASL to course offerings is also not likely to reach a broad enough audience to have a huge change, although it is great to have those options available.

61. C: To address weak areas, it is better to implement strategies that are backed by research and have been proven to yield good results. This can save the campus the time, effort, and resources that would be wasted if untested and unproven strategies were implemented unsuccessfully. When a leader is looking for strategies to foster change on campus, using research-based and proven best practices is beneficial because there will be a clear direction as to how to successfully implement the strategy and a realistic idea of what results to expect. When untested strategies are implemented, the outcome is less certain. Untested strategies also often take more research and a process of trial and error, or a learning curve, to implement, both of which can delay the implementation of change.

62. A: An emotionally safe environment is an environment where everyone can learn. It is free from all obstacles, negative emotions, and conflicts due to preventative strategies and quick resolutions. When an environment is not emotionally safe, children can feel fear, anxiety, and a host of other negative emotions. In an emotionally safe environment, both adults and children feel comfortable participating in the learning environment and interacting with one another. There is an absence of peer-to-peer conflict, peer-to-adult conflict, and bullying.

63. C: Although the fundamental American right to information access is important, it is not the only or most important factor in school acceptable use policies (AUPs). Some school districts require student agreement and parental permission forms for minor (under 18) students for independent electronic information use, but this is not always the case. Student intellectual freedom depends on their responsibility for accepting limits in that freedom. Experts do advise schools to contact electronic freedom of information organizations to inform themselves fully.

64. D: Professional development sessions that take place over time, in contrast to single-session trainings, are more likely to have an impact on teacher performance. Additionally, when a cohort of teachers participates in a training, there is opportunity for collaboration and collective accountability. There are benefits of providing individualized professional development opportunities for teachers. However, when these self-paced trainings are not time bound or

Copyright © Mometrix Media. You have been licensed one copy of this document for personal use only. Any other reproduction or redistribution is strictly prohibited. All rights reserved.
This content is provided for test preparation purposes only and does not imply an endorsement by Mometrix of any particular political, scientific, or religious point of view.

accompanied by accountability measures, they are less likely to have a direct impact on current teacher performance.

65. D: School leaders should not assign teachers to write technology standards. Integrating technology does help students meet curriculum standards. School leaders and faculty should require students to master any existing technology standards as cross-curricular and procedural knowledge and skills. Experts advise school leaders and teachers to focus not on learning about technology, but on learning with technology.

66. A: The school provides education and training to students that will make them employable in the community workforce. As a result, the school can supplement or adjust school programming to respond to the needs of the community, such as training students in particular employment fields that are experiencing a shortage within the community. Many schools, especially secondary schools, partner with their local community colleges and community organizations to identify employment trends in order to support the local community and increase the likelihood that graduates can obtain employment.

67. A: Summative assessment is assessment that is used to evaluate student learning for mastery. Summative assessment usually occurs at the end of an instructional unit or a designated period of time, such as a grading period or school year. These assessments are aligned to objectives or standards and are usually high stakes, which means they may count for a significant grade or may determine a student's progress in their educational career. A summative assessment may be a midterm or final exam, a research project, a unit test, or a standardized exam. The results of summative assessments may determine a student's grade promotion or earning of course credit. Results from summative assessments may also determine a school's performance according to accountability standards. Summative assessment results are often used by school leaders for instructional planning and goal setting for the subsequent school year.

68. B: The dean should ask teachers what resources they would like and purchase as many of their suggestions as possible for all teachers. This would increase the number of resources available to teachers and offer them a variety of resources to choose from. Requiring teachers to purchase materials on their own is a disincentive if teachers cannot afford the upfront cost. Professional development is not a resource, it is training. Seeking free or discounted materials does not guarantee that the number and variety of resources will increase on campus if there are limited to no resources available in the local area.

69. C: Analyzing videos of one's instructional practices is used in self-assessment and can also support reflection. Rather than relying on the observation feedback of a third party, the teacher can self-assess their proficiency in instructional delivery. Writing in a journal is used in reflection, not for self-assessment.

70. D: An effective school leader is transparent when making decisions. This transparency includes sharing data and/or rationale for making decisions. The school leader has already determined that the fine arts program should be discontinued so the best action for the principal to take next is to explain the rationale for that decision to the school community.

Constructed Response

1. Essay question graders commonly look for the following elements in a strong response: strong content knowledge, clear organization, and effective arguments or examples. Language and usage are not usually strictly graded, but can make a big impact on the clarity of your ideas.

Copyright © Mometrix Media. You have been licensed one copy of this document for personal use only. Any other reproduction or redistribution is strictly prohibited. All rights reserved.
This content is provided for test preparation purposes only and does not imply an endorsement by Mometrix of any particular political, scientific, or religious point of view.

Please use the provided rubric to make sure your response meets these common criteria. Try to have a friend or family member grade your response for you or take a break after writing your response and return to grade it with fresh eyes.

CONSTRUCTED RESPONSE RUBRIC

Domain	Description
Content Knowledge	• The response directly addresses every part of the prompt. • The response demonstrates independent knowledge of the topic. • The response discusses the topic at an appropriate depth.
Organization	• The response introduces the topic, usually with a thesis statement or by restating the prompt. • The response directly addresses the prompt by providing a clear and concise answer or solution. • The answer or solution is supported by logical arguments or evidence. • The response restates the main idea in the conclusion.
Arguments and Examples	• The response provides a reasonable answer to the prompt. • The answer is supported by strong reasoning or evidence. • The response develops ideas logically and connects ideas to one another. • The reasoning and evidence provided act to support a unified main idea.
Language and Usage	• The response demonstrates effective use of grammar and uses varied sentence structure throughout the response. • The response demonstrates correct use of spelling, punctuation, and capitalization. • The response demonstrates strong and varied use of vocabulary relevant to the topic and appropriate for the intended audience.

2. Essay question graders commonly look for the following elements in a strong response: strong content knowledge, clear organization, and effective arguments or examples. Language and usage are not usually strictly graded, but can make a big impact on the clarity of your ideas.

Please use the provided rubric to make sure your response meets these common criteria. Try to have a friend or family member grade your response for you or take a break after writing your response and return to grade it with fresh eyes.

Copyright © Mometrix Media. You have been licensed one copy of this document for personal use only. Any other reproduction or redistribution is strictly prohibited. All rights reserved.
This content is provided for test preparation purposes only and does not imply an endorsement by Mometrix of any particular political, scientific, or religious point of view.

Constructed Response Rubric

Domain	Description
Content Knowledge	• The response directly addresses every part of the prompt. • The response demonstrates independent knowledge of the topic. • The response discusses the topic at an appropriate depth.
Organization	• The response introduces the topic, usually with a thesis statement or by restating the prompt. • The response directly addresses the prompt by providing a clear and concise answer or solution. • The answer or solution is supported by logical arguments or evidence. • The response restates the main idea in the conclusion.
Arguments and Examples	• The response provides a reasonable answer to the prompt. • The answer is supported by strong reasoning or evidence. • The response develops ideas logically and connects ideas to one another. • The reasoning and evidence provided act to support a unified main idea.
Language and Usage	• The response demonstrates effective use of grammar and uses varied sentence structure throughout the response. • The response demonstrates correct use of spelling, punctuation, and capitalization. • The response demonstrates strong and varied use of vocabulary relevant to the topic and appropriate for the intended audience.

Copyright © Mometrix Media. You have been licensed one copy of this document for personal use only. Any other reproduction or redistribution is strictly prohibited. All rights reserved.
This content is provided for test preparation purposes only and does not imply an endorsement by Mometrix of any particular political, scientific, or religious point of view.

Practice Test #2

Multiple Choice Questions

1. Which of the following sources of data would be most beneficial for a school leader to analyze prior to developing or revising the school vision and goals?

a. Teacher turnover data, failure rates, and satisfaction survey results
b. Student performance data, student attendance data, and student promotion rates
c. Community engagement rates
d. School accountability ratings for the last three years

2. An elementary school leader has set a goal of establishing a school climate wherein all educators believe every child can learn and succeed, and are committed to enabling every child to do so. Which classroom practice should the leader encourage teachers to use toward this goal?

a. Differentiating instruction
b. Assigning student teams to compete in contests
c. Differentiating assessment standards by student
d. Regularly researching individual student interests

3. Which of the following is true about school leaders as role models for teachers in professional development (PD)?

a. School leaders should facilitate PD activities.
b. School leaders should participate in PD with teachers.
c. School leaders should monitor teacher implementation of learning from PD sessions.
d. School leaders should determine the PD offered to teachers.

4. Which of the following statements is most accurate about why schools must collaborate with their communities in providing mental health services to remove learning barriers and improve student outcomes?

a. In many communities and states, schools are often children's only mental health service providers.
b. Due to stigma associated with mental health needs, parents avoid familiar school settings and staff.
c. According to research study findings, students are less likely to seek counseling services in schools.
d. Mental health services in schools should be separated from mental health services in communities.

5. Which of the following statements does not support standardized classroom practices and procedures?

a. Improving the cost-efficiency of school programs by reducing differentiation
b. Increasing the conformity to curricula within departments
c. Promoting safety throughout the school
d. Ensuring that students can expect the same teaching style from each teacher

Copyright © Mometrix Media. You have been licensed one copy of this document for personal use only. Any other reproduction or redistribution is strictly prohibited. All rights reserved.
This content is provided for test preparation purposes only and does not imply an endorsement by Mometrix of any particular political, scientific, or religious point of view.

6. Which of the following is an appropriate example of an action that school leaders can take to change negative school cultures and employee attitudes that interfere with realizing school visions?

a. Observe indicators of school culture among students and staff.
b. Design professional development sessions for teachers that address school culture.
c. Frequently recount successful accomplishments of goals related to school vision.
d. Hold annual ceremonies for celebrating successes.

7. Which of the following statements is most accurate about how school leaders align school policies and practices with federal, state, district, and local school system policies?

a. State standardized assessment instruments are based solely on standards developed by states.
b. Individual schools directly apply state standards for developing their standardized assessments.
c. Schools directly reflect system standards, and yet ultimately are also aligned with federal policy.
d. Local school districts develop standardized assessments applying the federal standards directly.

8. The school principal informs the leadership team that she will participate in a six-week program to improve her leadership skills. This action best illustrates that:

a. The principal is a model for continuous professional growth.
b. The principal has weaknesses that need to be addressed.
c. The principal is self-reflective.
d. The principal is an effective leader.

9. Which of the following is true regarding how teacher evaluation standards should be designed?

a. Teacher evaluations should reference clear instructional standards to prioritize student learning.
b. Teacher evaluations should be conducted by school leaders with a single standardized measure.
c. Teacher evaluations should be based on occasional observation and avoid critical commentaries.
d. Teacher evaluations should play a minor part in important decisions about teacher employment.

10. What is most true about effective new teacher induction programs?

a. They should focus on supporting new teachers but not leaders.
b. They should give only new teachers professional development.
c. They should use self-assessments and reflection for teachers to measure performance.
d. They should improve student achievement via teacher efficacy.

Copyright © Mometrix Media. You have been licensed one copy of this document for personal use only. Any other reproduction or redistribution is strictly prohibited. All rights reserved.
This content is provided for test preparation purposes only and does not imply an endorsement by Mometrix of any particular political, scientific, or religious point of view.

11. According to research related to the factors that contribute to the success of higher-performing public schools, which of the following is true?

a. The school leader is the single defining success factor.
b. School success is based on a complex set of interrelated factors.
c. Schools cannot be successful without additional funding.
d. Factors related to curriculum and instruction are the most important determinants of success.

12. A middle school is expecting a dramatic increase in the number of students requiring special education services for the upcoming school year. Which of the following should be the principal's primary concern?

a. How this group of students will impact current student performance data
b. The availability of human and fiscal resources needed to meet the needs of this group of students
c. Community resources for this group of students
d. The reason for the increase in the number of students requiring special education

13. A school leader wants to become more involved in analyzing student work on campus. Which of the following actions should the school leader take to accomplish this goal?

a. Audit student work samples and discuss the student performance demonstrated with the teachers who assigned the work.
b. Monitor teacher grade books.
c. Host a science fair.
d. Mandate that teachers assess student learning using portfolios.

14. Which of the following statements is not accurate about requirements for integrating technology comprehensively into instruction to support school vision?

a. Successful school-wide implementation of educational technology is dependent on the technology selected, not school leadership.
b. Regardless of the technology capabilities of school staff, training and professional development are needed to successfully implement educational technology school-wide.
c. School structure and organization impact the success of adopting educational technology.
d. Schools must have the resources and support for implementing technology school-wide.

15. What must school leaders consider to mobilize and develop community school support?

a. Businesses and community-based organizations use the same language that educators use.
b. Exchanging and matching visions, missions, wants, and needs with stakeholders is sufficient.
c. Prospective community partners primarily want to know how collaboration benefits schools.
d. Prospective partner motivations are as varied as the organizations interested in partnership.

Copyright © Mometrix Media. You have been licensed one copy of this document for personal use only. Any other reproduction or redistribution is strictly prohibited. All rights reserved.
This content is provided for test preparation purposes only and does not imply an endorsement by Mometrix of any particular political, scientific, or religious point of view.

16. Which of the following is true regarding information and data that teachers should consider when planning for differentiated instruction?

a. Special population identification and past academic performance are the only data that teachers should consider when planning for differentiated instruction.
b. Formative assessment is not useful when planning for differentiated instruction.
c. Student interests should be a major determining factor when planning for differentiated instruction.
d. Student performance data, interests, and learning styles should all be considered when planning for differentiated instruction.

17. Experts find that, to build community capacity for contributing to school improvement, school leaders and staff must transcend traditional activities. What is true about how they can further continue community collaboration for school improvement?

a. For productive partnerships, schools should give stakeholders information only as they request it.
b. School leaders and staff should identify which community members can participate meaningfully.
c. All collaborations with community members should align directly with the campus vision and goals.
d. To engage and retain community partners, schools should limit the achievement data they share.

18. An elementary school principal serves at a school in which many of the parents of students speak little or no English. The language barrier creates challenges in communication, parent engagement, and the reinforcement of learning at home. Which of the following actions would best help the principal to address this challenge?

a. Hire a translator to communicate with parents.
b. Partner with an adult ESL program in the community and offer free ESL classes on campus.
c. Translate all school documents to the languages of the parents.
d. Ask students to translate information for their parents.

19. Which of the following represents the most effective way that a leader can ensure the staff members under their supervision act in an ethical manner?

a. Writing and distributing policies and procedures
b. Actively monitoring employee behavior
c. Requiring employees to sign a form to acknowledge receipt of the staff handbook
d. Responding to reports of unethical behavior immediately

20. A school leader has developed the vision and goals in collaboration with the campus leadership team and community stakeholders. Which of the following is the best step that the school leader should take next?

a. Develop a strategic plan for implementing the vision and goals.
b. Host a community meeting to present the vision and goals to all stakeholders.
c. Delegate tasks to leadership team members to implement the vision and goals.
d. Host a meeting with campus staff to present the vision and goals and inform them of their duties and responsibilities related to the vision and goals.

Copyright © Mometrix Media. You have been licensed one copy of this document for personal use only. Any other reproduction or redistribution is strictly prohibited. All rights reserved.
This content is provided for test preparation purposes only and does not imply an endorsement by Mometrix of any particular political, scientific, or religious point of view.

21. A middle school principal wants to improve the quality of teaching and learning on campus on a continuous basis throughout the school year rather than only reviewing annual performance data and making changes prior to the start of the school year. Which of the following strategies would best help the principal to achieve this goal?

a. Assess students every six weeks using benchmark exams and use the data to adjust the instructional program.
b. At the start of the school year, administer a comprehensive exam to determine what information students retained over the summer.
c. Administer a comprehensive exam to students at the beginning of the school year, in the middle of the school year, and at the end of the school year and use the data to make plans for the following school year.
d. Require that teachers maintain portfolios for all students to demonstrate learning and growth over the course of the school year.

22. All of the following demonstrate that the school leader conducts self-reflection EXCEPT:

a. Reading books and articles related to the field of education and leadership practice
b. Keeping a journal
c. Evaluating one's self using the personnel evaluation rubric
d. Attending a mandated training

23. Of the following, which is true about multiple assessments of student learning?

a. Different assessment types access different skills and learning styles.
b. Students must be re-tested often or they forget what they learned.
c. Summative assessments following instruction are typically sufficient.
d. Summative assessments enable adjusting instruction as it continues.

24. Among school leader responsibilities for managing daily school facility operations, which is MOST likely to involve district support for hiring expert consultants to address contemporary issues?

a. Managing the food services in the school
b. Managing school environmental quality
c. Managing school transportation services
d. Managing custodial services in a school

25. ABC Elementary School receives permission to participate in a television news media segment about keeping children active. The principal would like all of the students in the soccer club to participate in the filming of the news segment. What should the principal do first?

a. Inform the teachers that the media will be on campus.
b. Meet with the students to set expectations for behavior when they are being filmed.
c. Inform the community that the school will be participating in the news segment.
d. Ensure that all students who plan to participate have a media release form signed by a parent on file.

Copyright © Mometrix Media. You have been licensed one copy of this document for personal use only. Any other reproduction or redistribution is strictly prohibited. All rights reserved.
This content is provided for test preparation purposes only and does not imply an endorsement by Mometrix of any particular political, scientific, or religious point of view.

26. Which is a practice that national research studies find school leaders should *avoid* when speaking publicly and in other communication with key stakeholders?

a. Taking advantage of the political environment
b. Using commonly understood language with most audiences
c. Communicating in response to sensitive situations
d. Becoming engaged in large scale open forums

27. A principal has led the school in applying databases, word processing programs, spreadsheet programs, and other application software to solve problems, manage information, and create sophisticated products. This is most related to which purpose of technology use in schools?

a. Using technology as a productivity tool
b. Using technology as information access
c. Using technology as a cognitive stimulus
d. Using technology as instruction content

28. Which of the following is the best example of how school leaders can support teachers in developing their expertise and leadership skills?

a. School leaders should increase teachers' workloads to give them opportunity to demonstrate responsibility.
b. School leaders should develop all teachers in the same way to avoid building resentment among staff.
c. School leaders must create safe environments for teachers' risk-taking and creative ideas.
d. School leaders should limit how much authority to share with teachers to prevent diminishing their own authority.

29. The dean of instruction is preparing to implement an online literacy program that the school district has just purchased. Which feature of the literacy program platform best aligns with the school's mission to use data to make instructional decisions?

a. The program assesses students' reading levels bi-weekly.
b. The program tracks students' growth over time and compares their actual growth to expected growth.
c. The program autogenerates reports of student engagement and sends them to parents.
d. The program provides all teachers and administrators with access to a data dashboard that includes all data collected through the program.

30. Regarding school buildings and grounds maintenance, for which of these are school leaders directly responsible?

a. Inspection and maintenance procedure development
b. Allocation of budget for inspection and maintenance
c. Inspection and maintenance schedules development
d. Preventive maintenance procedures implementation

31. What is the most accurate definition of a learning objective?

a. What educators hope to accomplish during their instruction
b. What educators are supposed instruct the students
c. What students expect teachers to instruct them
d. What educators expect students to be able to do via instruction

Copyright © Mometrix Media. You have been licensed one copy of this document for personal use only. Any other reproduction or redistribution is strictly prohibited. All rights reserved.
This content is provided for test preparation purposes only and does not imply an endorsement by Mometrix of any particular political, scientific, or religious point of view.

32. Which of the following is correct about effective classroom management systems?

a. Tiered positive behavior support models provide both prevention and intervention.
b. Tiered positive behavior support models are only for preventing behavior problems.
c. Tiered positive behavior support models are designed to be behavior interventions.
d. Tiered positive behavior support models provide less time in academic engagement.

33. The first year of a mentoring pilot program has been completed. The first year was free for the school, but the school will have to pay a fee if the mentoring program is to continue for subsequent years. Which of the following would best inform the principal's decision about whether to continue the program?

a. The number of students who participated in the program
b. Student feedback on the program
c. Community feedback on the program
d. Student performance indicators related to the campus goals

34. Which of the following is most accurate about effective and appropriate school and co-curricular activities to prepare high school students for college and careers?

a. Career and technical education can only be obtained in magnet or technical schools.
b. School partnerships with higher education institutions best prepare students for jobs.
c. Community-based and project-based learning prepare students for higher education.
d. High school curricula should be pertinent to student lives, communities, and cultures.

35. Which of the following accurately describes cognitive and affective processes involved in school organizational learning and staff development?

a. Conversation and affirmation are cognitive; reflection and invitation are affective
b. Reflection and conversation are cognitive; affirmation and invitation are affective
c. Reflection and affirmation are cognitive; conversation and invitation are affective
d. Affirmation and invitation are cognitive; reflection and conversation are affective

36. Which of the following is true about mental health and student learning and achievement?

a. Educational problems are not related to mental health issues.
b. External stressors can create obstacles to learning and achievement.
c. Only psychological disorders diagnosed by a health professional can be addressed in schools.
d. Only students who qualify for special education services can receive support for mental health issues.

37. Which statement is accurate about why classroom management systems are effective?

a. By making learning environments orderly, they enable student academic success.
b. They control student behavior rather than helping emotional-social development.
c. They work by increasing prosocial behavior rather than academic engagement.
d. They work by providing individualized intensive interventions for all students.

Copyright © Mometrix Media. You have been licensed one copy of this document for personal use only. Any other reproduction or redistribution is strictly prohibited. All rights reserved.
This content is provided for test preparation purposes only and does not imply an endorsement by Mometrix of any particular political, scientific, or religious point of view.

38. According to multiple research studies, what is a characteristic of school leaders related to evaluating teacher effectiveness?

a. The most effective school leaders are better at identifying the best candidates for hiring as teachers.
b. The most effective school leaders are better at identifying the best and worst teachers on their staff.
c. The most effective teachers are attracted to the schools whose leaders have hired the best teachers.
d. The most effective school leaders are better at identifying excellent and average teachers than poorer ones.

39. For managing school food services, the FDA refers to seven Hazard Analysis and Critical Control Point (HACCP) principles. Which of the following lists these principles in the correct sequence?

a. Identifying CCPs, determining critical limits to control hazards, hazard analysis, planning corrective actions, establishing CCP monitoring procedures, record-keeping system, verification procedures.
b. Hazard analysis, identifying CCPs, determining critical limits to control hazards, establishing CCP monitoring procedures, planning corrective actions, verification procedures, record-keeping system.
c. Verification procedures, determining critical limits to control hazards, identifying CCPs, establishing CCP monitoring procedures, hazard analysis, record-keeping system, planning corrective actions.
d. Determining critical limits to control hazards, identifying CCPs, establishing CCP monitoring procedures, verification procedures, record-keeping system, planning corrective actions, hazard analysis.

40. A parent of a student with a disability informs the principal that they overheard two teachers making fun of their child's disability during dismissal. Which of the following is the most appropriate response that the principal should make to the parent?

a. Inform the parent that they have permission to pick their child up from school early.
b. Inform the parent that the teachers will be disciplined.
c. Assure the parent that the described behavior is not tolerated, and an investigation will occur.
d. Assure the parent that the teachers will no longer have dismissal duty.

41. How should school leaders and others analyze school data to inform the school vision?

a. Across grade levels instead of across school years
b. By subject matter rather than by student cohorts
c. By formative and summative assessment findings
d. By teachers within grades instead of across levels

42. A school principal would like to develop a positive partnership with the school community. Which of the following actions would best help the principal to achieve this goal?

a. Publish a monthly school newsletter with reminders for important school events.
b. Host a student award ceremony each semester to highlight school and student successes.
c. Attend all school athletic events.
d. Send a survey to all community members to get their feedback on school performance.

Copyright © Mometrix Media. You have been licensed one copy of this document for personal use only. Any other reproduction or redistribution is strictly prohibited. All rights reserved.
This content is provided for test preparation purposes only and does not imply an endorsement by Mometrix of any particular political, scientific, or religious point of view.

43. The athletics director received notice that there will be random drug testing of all student athletes next week. The principal discovers that the athletics director acted against policy and advised all of the coaches to inform students of the upcoming drug test. Which of the following actions should the principal take next?

a. Give the athletics director a written reprimand for breaching policy.
b. Document the infraction in the athletics director's personnel file.
c. Inform the athletics department of the information breach.
d. Remove the athletics director from his or her position.

44. In school-wide positive behavior support (SPBS) programs, which of the following is a procedure associated with tier 3?

a. Socio-emotional groups
b. Daily check-in and check-out
c. Intervention family support
d. Individualized interventions

Refer to the following for question 45:

The school principal reviews classroom observation and feedback with assistant principals weekly but often has very few classroom observations of their own conducted in preparation for the weekly meeting. This week, a teacher complained to the principal that the feedback from their most recent evaluation was not fair because it did not provide a well-rounded view of their performance.

45. What action should the school principal take to increase the frequency of classroom visits?

a. Make a commitment to visit classrooms every morning before the day gets too busy.
b. Clear their schedule on a specific day of the week to dedicate to classroom visits.
c. Plan out the classrooms that should be visited for the week and add them to the calendar with reminders.
d. Carry classroom observation forms at all times and visit classrooms when an opportunity presents itself.

46. Surveyed school principals have reported that which of the following has been adversely affected since standards-based accountability systems were implemented?

a. Teacher morale
b. Curriculum and instruction
c. Student assessment practices
d. Expectations and achievement

47. Advanced technology integration in schools includes empowering students to engage in the learning process using technology. Which of the following best exemplifies students creating content using digital media?

a. Students access wiki pages to review lesson materials.
b. Students record themselves reading aloud for reading assessment.
c. Students design elaborate digital storybooks to prepare for a state writing exam.
d. Students create PowerPoint presentations about insects using photos from the Internet.

Copyright © Mometrix Media. You have been licensed one copy of this document for personal use only. Any other reproduction or redistribution is strictly prohibited. All rights reserved.
This content is provided for test preparation purposes only and does not imply an endorsement by Mometrix of any particular political, scientific, or religious point of view.

48. Which of the following is the least effective way that school leaders can create inclusive school communities?

a. Encourage students whose parents do not speak English to translate for them when interacting with school staff.
b. Provide video recordings and resources to parents who miss workshops and meetings.
c. Validate, honor, and thank family and community for supporting the school.
d. Hire parent liaisons to help parents access resources and services offered by the school.

49. Leadership is one of the factors identified by research as instrumental in implementing school-wide technology adoption. This includes multiple roles for school leaders. Which set of responsibilities is associated with the role of learning organization leader?

a. Making change a priority, supporting and encouraging teacher endeavors
b. Making sure that teachers have what they need to meet goals for change
c. Setting high learning and collaborative standards as conditions for change
d. Leading initiatives, resolving problems, and providing learning opportunities for faculty

50. The federal Supportive School Discipline Initiative (SSDI) issued a (2014) positive school discipline guidance package. Why did the US Department of Justice (DOJ) collaborate with the US Department of Education (ED) in producing this resource?

a. To make school discipline consistent with justice and correctional systems
b. To address inevitable student justice involvement by disciplinary exclusion
c. To ensure that Civil Rights Act titles prohibiting discrimination are enforced
d. To establish disciplinary practices to keep juvenile offenders out of school

51. Which of the following strategies is least likely to improve teacher practice?

a. Conducting regular classroom observations and providing written feedback to teachers
b. Pairing novice teachers with an experienced teacher for peer coaching
c. Providing teachers with aggregated student performance data each grading cycle
d. Facilitating professional learning communities for teacher collaboration by grade level and by content area

52. Which of the following is a primary benefit of distributed leadership?

a. Distributed leadership helps to maintain status quo, especially in high-performing schools.
b. School leaders who practice distributive leadership are less stressed because they are able to delegate responsibilities.
c. Practicing distributive leadership builds capacity in others and develops followers into leaders.
d. Distributive leadership helps to identify weak team members that need to be replaced.

53. A high school principal is concerned that ninth-grade students who read below grade level are not performing well on benchmark tests in reading and writing. Which of the following steps should the principal take to best address this concern?

a. Provide test preparation sessions for these students after school and on weekends and monitor student attendance to the sessions.
b. Integrate reading and writing skills into all subject areas and provide training to all teachers on fundamental reading strategies.
c. Increase the opportunities that students have to spend in the school library.
d. Purchase a reading software program that students can use at home.

Copyright © Mometrix Media. You have been licensed one copy of this document for personal use only. Any other reproduction or redistribution is strictly prohibited. All rights reserved.
This content is provided for test preparation purposes only and does not imply an endorsement by Mometrix of any particular political, scientific, or religious point of view.

54. Which of these is true regarding school leader efforts involving school improvement plans, policies, and structures to improve parent engagement, student engagement, and student achievement?

a. School improvement plans increased parental meeting attendance but not student school attendance.
b. School improvement plans decreased student behavior problems while increasing their achievement.
c. Central office policies and structures increased parent engagement in individual schools, not systems.
d. School improvement plans increased student enrollment and achievement, not parent involvement.

55. Which kind of data best helps teachers to identify strengths and needs in their teaching practices, support capacity-building, and identify specific remedial student groups?

a. Formative data
b. Summative data
c. Student profiles
d. Enrollment data

56. Which of the following is accurate about the uses of data in goal-related activities?

a. Qualitative data is not useful when setting goals aligned with school vision and mission.
b. Data connected to vision and mission enable monitoring progress for goals.
c. Only formative data is relevant to how schools allocate resources to meet their goals.
d. Formal data collection is not necessary to assess family and community relations.

57. In a school's Acceptable Use Policy (AUP) for classroom Internet technology, which section is MOST likely to cross-reference or even duplicate the general school disciplinary code?

a. Violations and sanctions
b. Acceptable uses
c. Unacceptable uses
d. Policy statement

58. Which of the following is true about the efficacy of new teacher induction programs on schools?

a. They make new teachers more comfortable, not more effective.
b. They increase the rates at which the new teachers are retained.
c. They enhance teacher instructional skills, not teacher leadership.
d. They help education inequities more than student achievement.

Copyright © Mometrix Media. You have been licensed one copy of this document for personal use only. Any other reproduction or redistribution is strictly prohibited. All rights reserved.
This content is provided for test preparation purposes only and does not imply an endorsement by Mometrix of any particular political, scientific, or religious point of view.

59. Which of the following actions best demonstrates a middle school leader monitoring instructional practices and student progress to ensure that all students are prepared for a challenging curriculum?

a. Offering a summer bridge program for underperforming seventh-grade students entering eighth-grade.
b. Reviewing the performance of incoming sixth-grade students on standardized tests.
c. Evaluating the course grades of eighth-grade students enrolled in an Algebra I course for high school credit.
d. Comparing student performance on standardized tests to course grades to determine alignment of assessment.

60. School leaders must know of a wide range of mental health professionals available to students. To which of the following are students most often referred for help that schools cannot provide?

a. Career counselors
b. Family counselors
c. Group counselors
d. School counselors

Refer to the following for question 61:

The school principal reviews classroom observation and feedback with assistant principals weekly but often has very few classroom observations of their own conducted in preparation for the weekly meeting. This week, a teacher complained to the principal that the feedback from their most recent evaluation was not fair because it did not provide a well-rounded view of their performance.

61. When increasing the frequency of classroom visits, which of the following should NOT be considered when the school principal observes teachers in their classrooms?

a. The quality and rigor of assignments given to students.
b. The implementation of strategies learned in professional development sessions.
c. Classroom environment and culture.
d. The teacher's tenure or contract status.

62. Challenges to school leaders for promoting student mental health include limited resources. Among such limitations, which is most related to federal accountability mandates?

a. Ratios of school counselors to students
b. School counselor responsibility change
c. Inadequate support staff development
d. Districts' mental health staff budgeting

Copyright © Mometrix Media. You have been licensed one copy of this document for personal use only. Any other reproduction or redistribution is strictly prohibited. All rights reserved.
This content is provided for test preparation purposes only and does not imply an endorsement by Mometrix of any particular political, scientific, or religious point of view.

63. To evaluate teacher effectiveness in applying instructional strategies, school leaders need a working knowledge of student-centered, research-based teaching methods. What is most true about these?

a. The Socratic method is a useful, research-based strategy for delivering instruction.
b. Project-based learning requires technology integration in order to be implemented effectively.
c. Cooperative learning has been proven to be an effective, research-based instructional strategy.
d. It is necessary for teachers to utilize technology to deliver instruction in order to be effective.

64. Which of the following is NOT true about the qualifications of teachers in public schools?

a. Teachers must be fully-certified to teach in a public school.
b. Teachers must be highly-qualified to teach in a public school.
c. A teacher who moves states may have to demonstrate subject-matter competency in the new state to teach.
d. Teachers in high-performing schools generally have more qualifications than teachers in other public schools.

65. The school participates in a health education program that provides sex education and contraceptives to middle school students. A teacher is opposed to this program and becomes very vocal in the community about the dangers of having this program on campus. The principal begins to receive numerous phone calls and emails about the program. Which of the following actions would best help the principal refocus attention to vision and goals?

a. Issue a public statement regarding the value of health education and the alignment of the program with the school's vision.
b. Meet with the teacher who is opposed to the program to reach an agreement.
c. Ignore the phone calls and emails.
d. Hold a community meeting to discuss the program with stakeholders.

66. The sixth-grade math department meets as a professional learning community and determines that overall students in sixth-grade are not performing well on the same three math objectives. However, these same students are performing satisfactorily on other math objectives. Which of the following is the most likely reason that the sixth-grade students are not mastering the identified math objectives?

a. The math teachers are ineffective in teaching the identified math objectives.
b. The curriculum is not properly aligned to address the identified math objectives.
c. The students need additional tutoring to master the identified math objectives.
d. The assessment used to measure student performance was biased.

67. In public school districts, which personnel are *not* likely to be directly supervised by the campus principal?

a. Bus drivers
b. Custodians
c. Volunteers
d. Cafeteria workers

Copyright © Mometrix Media. You have been licensed one copy of this document for personal use only. Any other reproduction or redistribution is strictly prohibited. All rights reserved.
This content is provided for test preparation purposes only and does not imply an endorsement by Mometrix of any particular political, scientific, or religious point of view.

68. Of the following, which is an advantage of developing a school vision collaboratively?

a. Visions developed through collaboration can be implemented far faster.
b. Visions are clearer and more coherent when developed by collaboration.
c. Visions take longer times in the process of development, slowing change.
d. Visions tend to be more appropriate to their local school district contexts.

69. In school change processes, which of these is an example of a first-order change?

a. Forming a different approach to instruction
b. Forming new interactions and relationships
c. Forming site-based school advisory councils
d. Forming a sense of collaborative ownership

70. Which of the following best describes how the school leader should evaluate the technology data systems they use?

a. Does the data system provide the data necessary to support the work of collaborative data teams?
b. Is the technology data system affordable?
c. Is the technology data system user friendly?
d. Do other schools use this technology data system?

Constructed Response

1. You are the principal of an 1800-student urban high school with a primarily African-American and Hispanic/Latino student population. The school has an active student newspaper with a much-beloved journalism teacher. Over the past several months, the student-staff have published several items of dubious origin that have caused controversy in the larger community. These items have typically had topics dealing with race relations. You have spoken to the journalism teacher after each incident about not allowing students to publish this type of questionable content. The newest issue of the student newspaper contains another such item. In 150-300 words, describe what you would do to address the situation.

2. You are the new principal of a 700-student elementary (K-5) school. The previous principal left the school in the midst of some controversy and there has been a significant turnover in teaching staff. In your first couple of weeks on the job, you notice a considerable amount of negativity among staff, in large part fomented by teachers who have been at the school for several years and have had multiple principals. In 300-600 words describe the strategies that you would use to address this negativity and change the culture of the school to a more positive tone and improve teacher and staff morale.

Copyright © Mometrix Media. You have been licensed one copy of this document for personal use only. Any other reproduction or redistribution is strictly prohibited. All rights reserved.
This content is provided for test preparation purposes only and does not imply an endorsement by Mometrix of any particular political, scientific, or religious point of view.

Answer Key and Explanations for Test #2

Multiple Choice Questions

1. B: All of the data mentioned would be useful for the school leader to analyze; however, data related to student performance, student attendance data, and student promotion rates are the most comprehensive and informative for the development or revision of the school vision and goals. This data can assist in developing goals that are aligned with federal and state accountability requirements. Analyzing data related to teaching staff and the community are important for understanding and improving campus culture and supporting the instructional goals, but are not the most beneficial when compared to student data. Similarly, school accountability ratings can be helpful to analyze but do not provide sufficient information related to current practice and to the areas of deficit that need to be addressed in the school goals.

2. A: Implementing differentiated instruction helps teachers to meet students where they are based on performance, learning style, and other student characteristics. Instruction can be differentiated based on lesson delivery, student activities, and student assessment. However, standards are often standardized and must remain the same for students as all students are expected to learn and succeed. Teachers can provide individualized resources and support to help students to meet those needs.

3. B: Research finds that school leader participation in PD is what determines teacher and school-wide participation in PD. School leaders set an example for teachers by actively engaging in the PD that teachers are expected to engage in. School leaders should have a vision for PD offerings but can empower teachers to choose PD offerings that meet their needs. School leaders can facilitate PD activities but should also allow teacher leaders to facilitate PD as well. School leaders should monitor implementation of PD but this activity is not directly related to being a role model for teachers.

4. A: In many American communities and states, schools provide the chief—and often the only—mental health (MH) services that children receive. Parents are more comfortable with such services when they are provided in familiar school settings by familiar staff, rather than avoiding them. Research studies find students are *more* likely to seek counseling services in schools than to look elsewhere. Another reason for school-community collaboration is the necessity of coordinating school and community MH services, not separating them.

5. D: Reducing the teachers' teaching styles is not a priority if the teacher is effective at achieving standards in the curriculum. Reducing variability in classrooms throughout the school tends to promote efficiency in purchasing, and in producing testing materials, since each department can use the same materials. This also could allow for benchmarking from class to class, which helps with pacing the curriculum throughout the year. Other procedures and policies, such as bathroom policies or electronic device policies can promote safety by making sure each student is accounted for.

6. C: School leaders should frequently highlight successes related to accomplishing the school vision to show stakeholders that the vision is viable and successful. Ceremonies for celebrating successes and other ways of highlighting successes are beneficial but must be conducted frequently in order to change a negative school culture. Providing professional development for teachers related to culture can be beneficial but would not address issues with culture for all employees on

Copyright © Mometrix Media. You have been licensed one copy of this document for personal use only. Any other reproduction or redistribution is strictly prohibited. All rights reserved.
This content is provided for test preparation purposes only and does not imply an endorsement by Mometrix of any particular political, scientific, or religious point of view.

campus. Additionally, it is important for leaders to make observations about school culture, but observations without action will not positively impact school culture.

7. C: All levels, from individual schools to state education departments, must ultimately align with federal policy to make major educational goals match the national vision. However, within this hierarchy, specific expressions of policy, e.g., standardized test instruments, reflect the next higher level. Thus, state standardized tests reflect federal standards, not just state standards; individual schools *directly* apply standards from their school systems, not state standards, which in turn reflect the standards of their school districts, which in turn *directly* apply state standards, not federal standards.

8. A: The principal's announcement that they are committing to an ongoing training program indicates that they are committed to professional growth. This is a model to the other members of the leadership team.

9. A: According to the New Teacher Project (2011), design standards for effective teacher evaluation systems include evaluating teachers a minimum of once yearly, using multiple levels (4 or 5) for rating teachers, basing evaluations on clear instructional excellence standards prioritizing student learning, using multiple performance measures emphasizing teacher impact on student academic progress, making frequent observations and giving critical and/or constructive feedback, and making evaluation outcomes significant by using them as a major factor in important teacher employment decisions.

10. D: Effective new teacher induction programs should focus on supporting not only the new teachers, but also the school leaders who guide them. This requires offering professional development not only to new teachers, but equally to their mentors, school leaders, and other site leaders. Effective induction programs use research-based and standards-based assessment instruments to assess and inform new teacher performance. The ultimate goal of teacher induction programs that make teachers more effective is to improve student achievement.

11. B: Researchers found that, among public schools, those with higher performance than others each seemed to have a unique combination of factors contributing to their success. These factors include having a clear and shared focus, having high expectations and standards for students, and high levels of family and community involvement. An effective school leader is a significant factor in high performing schools but is not the only determinant of success. Similarly, alignment of curriculum and instruction and frequent monitoring of teaching and learning are critical success factors but cannot be deemed the most important. Finally, schools need resources for success, but many public schools have demonstrated success with meager funding.

12. B: Although the principal should be concerned with a variety of ways that this influx of students may impact the current instructional program, the primary concern should be how equipped the school is to provide this special population of students with an appropriate education. Human resources may include teachers and paraprofessionals. Fiscal resources may include furniture, equipment, technology, and other physical resources needed to support instruction.

13. A: The school leader should make time to collect and analyze student work samples. The audit can be random or the school leader can focus on particular groups of students based on data. However, the school leader should discuss the work samples with the teachers who assigned them. Monitoring grades does not provide the school leader with information about the assignments that were graded. Hosting a science fair and using portfolios for assessment can be beneficial but do not directly indicate that the school leader is involved in these activities.

Copyright © Mometrix Media. You have been licensed one copy of this document for personal use only. Any other reproduction or redistribution is strictly prohibited. All rights reserved.
This content is provided for test preparation purposes only and does not imply an endorsement by Mometrix of any particular political, scientific, or religious point of view.

14. A: Research studies find that, for implementing school-wide technology adoption, required factors are sufficient resources and support, professional development, school structure, school organization, and leadership. Effective professional development must be intentionally and carefully planned, designed with goals in mind, provided continually to keep up with constant changes in the teaching profession, and integrated system-wide or school-wide as part of the school culture through teacher collaboration and sharing of knowledge.

15. D: To mobilize and develop community school support, school leaders should consider that businesses and community-based organizations use different language than educators, and should learn and speak their languages accordingly. School leaders must not only exchange their visions, missions, wants, and needs with those of prospective community partners and identify where these match, they must moreover identify where they overlap, i.e., shared commonalities despite differences. School leaders must show prospective partners how collaboration benefits them. Potential partners have motivations as varied as the community organizations interested in collaborating with schools.

16. D: When planning for differentiated instruction, teachers should utilize as much data as possible that can be useful in determining how students can best learn. Identification in special populations such as special education, English as second language, gifted and talented, and others are helpful when planning differentiated instruction but are not the only factors to be considered. Student interests, learning styles, formative and summative data, and other relevant data should all be considered when planning differentiated instruction.

17. C: To partner productively with community members for the shared goal of improving student learning and achievement, schools should take the initiative in offering them information (including school and student data) rather than furnish it only upon request, clearly explain to stakeholders how *all* community members can participate meaningfully, align all collaborative activities directly with the school's vision and goals, and share pertinent, accurate, clear achievement data transparently rather than limiting what they disclose.

18. B: The action that would best address the challenges in communication, parental engagement, and at home learning is to help the parents learn English by offering ESL classes on campus. Hosting the classes on campus encourages parents to engage with the school community and reinforces that the school values the presence and engagement of the parents. Having a translator on campus and translating documents for parents are important actions to take but are not long-term solutions to the challenge. Students should not be asked to translate school information for their parents.

19. B: The best way to ensure that others are acting ethically is to actively monitor employee behavior. This can be done in person by walking around and observing performance, instructing others on the leadership team to observe employee behavior, and monitoring using security cameras. Security cameras are useful in areas that are most prone to unethical conduct, such as places where money is exchanged, entrances and exits, records storage, and areas on campus that are not frequently trafficked. While it is recommended to have policies and procedures for ethical behavior in place, the school leader must actively monitor adherence to those policies and procedures.

20. A: The next step after developing the school vision and goals is to develop a plan for implementing them. The plan should be developed prior to presenting the vision and goals to staff and other stakeholders so that, when they are presented, these stakeholders can be informed of their roles and responsibilities related to implementation of the vision and goals. It is important for

Copyright © Mometrix Media. You have been licensed one copy of this document for personal use only. Any other reproduction or redistribution is strictly prohibited. All rights reserved.
This content is provided for test preparation purposes only and does not imply an endorsement by Mometrix of any particular political, scientific, or religious point of view.

a school leader to delegate tasks to other leaders on campus in relation to the vision and goals, but the plan must be developed first for the leader to know which tasks to delegate.

21. A: The best strategy the principal can use to establish a continuous improvement cycle is to assess students at regular intervals and adjust instruction based on the data. Benchmark exams are typically shorter assessments over selected objectives rather than large comprehensive assessments. Data from these assessments reflect the mastery of objectives that are recently taught and are aligned to the pacing of the curriculum scope and sequence. Testing in less frequent intervals can also be helpful if the data is used to adjust instruction immediately rather than informing plans for the subsequent school year.

22. D: Attending a mandated training session indicates that the leader failed to identify that the training was needed for themselves, but instead needed to be directed by someone else to attend. Self-reflection involves reflecting on one's own performance in comparison to a set of leadership expectations and standards.

23. A: Individual students have different learning styles, skills, strengths, and weaknesses, so it is important to administer multiple and varied assessments to assemble as comprehensive a picture as possible of each student's existing knowledge, new learning, and instructional needs. Multiple assessments are not used to keep students from forgetting. Summative assessments following instruction are not sufficient as they do not continuously assess student learning and progress, and they do not enable teachers to adjust ongoing instruction to be more effective as formative assessments made during instruction do.

24. B: In recent decades, environmental quality issues have emerged that affect school facility operations management. These include asbestos, radon, and other hazardous materials control; energy conservation; and improvement of water, indoor air quality, and acoustics, which may all involve district support in hiring expert facility consultants. Since school leaders have government guidelines with school policies and procedures already in place for food services (A); transportation (C) and custodial (D) services that have existed longer than environmental awareness, they are less likely to require expert consultation.

25. D: Many school districts require parents to provide express permission for their child to appear in photographs and videos for media purposes. Other school districts indicate that consent is implied unless there is written documentation expressly forbidding their child to appear in content for media. In either circumstance, the school leader needs to confirm that each student who will participate has permission from a parent or guardian to do so.

26. D: According to the National Center for Education Statistics (NCES), school leaders should *not* ignore the political environment because political support and connections can greatly benefit obtaining funding and legislation. They should avoid overly technical language with most stakeholder audiences who will not understand industry jargon. Leaders should communicate with stakeholders in sensitive situations. However, leaders should avoid engaging in large-scale open forums which can obstruct progress by being unfocused, unstructured, and may admit too many voices.

27. A: Experts have identified four purposes of school technology use: productivity, information access, cognitive stimulus, and instruction content. Databases, word processing programs, spreadsheet programs, and other application software can all be classified as productivity tools. Applying these tools to problem solving and information management is an example of using technology as a productivity tool. Using technology as information involves the Internet and

Copyright © Mometrix Media. You have been licensed one copy of this document for personal use only. Any other reproduction or redistribution is strictly prohibited. All rights reserved.
This content is provided for test preparation purposes only and does not imply an endorsement by Mometrix of any particular political, scientific, or religious point of view.

associated information technologies; as a cognitive stimulus involves giving students real-life experiences and authentic simulations to extend learning and stimulate cognitive development; and as instructional content by employing advanced digital content for teaching, drilling, and practicing.

28. C: To encourage teacher leadership, school leaders must create safe environments wherein teachers can take risks and think creatively. School leaders should share authority with teachers to assist them in developing leadership skills and demonstrate responsibility. Increasing a teacher's workload with work that is not directly related to increased responsibilities or to skill refinement is not an example of developing a teacher. Additionally, leaders must differentiate support for teachers based on the current performance, skill, and attitudes.

29. D: The online literacy program collects valuable data, but the data must be accessible by instructional decision makers for them to be able to make data-driven instructional decisions. Collecting data without being able to access it is not effective for data-driven decision making. In order for data to be useful, it must be easily accessible by those who need it in a timely manner. In this scenario, teachers and administrators would be able to access all the data in one location, which would facilitate using that data to make decisions using that data.

30. B: School leaders are directly responsible for allocating budget for school maintenance and inspections. They should assign experienced maintenance supervisors to develop specific inspection and maintenance procedures (A) and schedules (C) and should oversee the implementation of preventive maintenance procedures, which they cannot directly implement by themselves (D).

31. D: Learning objectives are not what educators hope to accomplish, want to teach students, or what students expect teachers to impart to them. Instead, they are what educators expect their students to be able to do after they have instructed them in a content subject lesson, unit, or course. Experts observe that a common teacher error is to misinterpret learning objectives as things they plan to do during instruction instead of what they will expect students to do following instruction.

32. A: Tiered positive behavior support models have been found highly effective as school-wide classroom management systems because they incorporate not only prevention of behavior problems before they occur, but also interventions for existing or developing behavior problems. Also, by reducing the incidence of problem behaviors, these models provide *more* time for students to be engaged academically.

33. D: Although the other sources of information can be helpful, the principal must ensure that all funds allotted in the school budget are aligned with the campus vision and goals. When school funds are utilized, there must be a return on the investment that aligns with the vision and goals for the school. Programs and resources that do not align with the school vision and goals must be deprioritized or even eliminated.

34. D: To help students prepare for their futures, high schools should design curricula relevant to students' lives, communities, and cultural milieus. This includes the career and technical education they will need for today's world, which public high schools must offer. School partnerships with colleges and universities best prepare students for higher education, while community-based and project-based learning best prepare students for employment.

35. B: According to researchers (Mitchell and Sackney, 1998), both reflection (i.e., considering their own practices) and conversation (i.e., discussing their and colleagues' practices) enable teachers to have awareness of their own and others' practices, evaluate them, and discover possible alternatives. These are cognitive processes. Affirmation of one another as professionals, and

Copyright © Mometrix Media. You have been licensed one copy of this document for personal use only. Any other reproduction or redistribution is strictly prohibited. All rights reserved.
This content is provided for test preparation purposes only and does not imply an endorsement by Mometrix of any particular political, scientific, or religious point of view.

invitation into school decision-making both validate all staff members' contributions, acknowledge individual professional competencies, and thereby establish positive working relationships. These are affective processes.

36. B: External stressors can create short-term or long-term obstacles for student learning and achievement and can lead to or be evidence of mental health issues. Not all student mental health issues or crises carry an official diagnosis; however, educators can provide support and resources for the symptoms that students display. Furthermore, students with diagnosed mental health issues may be provided support and resources through a 504-education plan in addition to or in lieu of an individualized education plan. Additionally, educators can offer resources and support to students with mental health issues who do not receive services under either program.

37. A: Classroom management systems, e.g., tiered school-wide positive behavior support systems, make learning environments orderly, enabling students to learn more easily and succeed academically. Rather than only controlling student behavior, they foster and sustain appropriate classroom behavior while also promoting student emotional and social development. They are effective for increasing both prosocial behavior and academic engagement in students. By providing universal supports in the first-tier school-wide, they succeed for 80-85% of students, while individualized intensive interventions are reserved for the remaining 15-20% in the third tier.

38. B: Multiple research studies find that the most effective school leaders are better at identifying the teachers best and worst at increasing student performance among their existing faculty. However, researchers cannot determine whether the fact that effective school leaders also hire the best experienced teachers is more attributable to better leader ability in choosing teachers or to excellent teachers' attraction to schools with the best existing faculty quality. Researchers do observe that school leaders cannot differentiate quality among average teachers as well as they can differentiate better from poorer teachers due to lesser contrast.

39. B: Hazard analysis: analyzing food service operation and determining likely food safety hazards and control measures. Identifying CCPs: identifying those few control measures absolutely essential to food safety. Determining critical limits: cooking temperatures, times, and other observable and measurable safety-defining boundaries. Establishing CCP monitoring procedures: tracking CCP control as food flows through operations. Planning corrective actions: planning what to do when a critical limit at a CCP is not met and communicating to and training employees in preventive decisions. Verification procedures: ensuring a scientifically sound system for effective hazard control. Record-keeping system: documenting the HACCP system and plan.

40. C: The school leader's responsibility is to investigate the accusation that has been made to determine next steps. An investigation is needed because the school leader cannot take immediate action in response to the teachers' actions based solely on the report of the parent. Whether the teachers will be disciplined or not, the school leader should not discuss such discipline of personnel with others.

41. C: School leaders and others should analyze school data based upon formative classroom assessments and standardized state summative assessments. The data analyzed should include data across grade levels, across school years, by subjects, by student cohorts, by student special populations, and by individual teachers, when possible. Analysis of data should be holistic in order to identify school strengths, needs for improvement, and trends to properly inform the school vision and mission.

Copyright © Mometrix Media. You have been licensed one copy of this document for personal use only. Any other reproduction or redistribution is strictly prohibited. All rights reserved.
This content is provided for test preparation purposes only and does not imply an endorsement by Mometrix of any particular political, scientific, or religious point of view.

42. B: Recognizing and celebrating educational success is an effective strategy to develop positive family and community partnerships. A school leader should make an effort to organize events on campus and in the community to develop positive partnerships. Live events facilitate two-way communication, unlike newsletters which are one-way modes of communication. Attending athletic events and soliciting feedback from the community are additional ways to build a relationship with the community, but the most effective strategy for building a positive partnership is to host an event that spotlights positive things related to the school and students.

43. A: The athletic director acted inappropriately by breaching confidential information. As a result, the drug testing plan will need to be revised and some level of disciplinary procedures should take place. This breach of information should be handled officially and documented in the event that more issues arise later on. The infraction is not a personal matter, but is one dealing with breach of policy, so this should be made into an official written reprimand (choice A), rather than as a note in a personnel file (choice B). Finally, assuming this is the first major offense by the athletic director, the offense is not likely to be so consequential that the athletic director should be removed from his or her position as in choice D.

44. D: In SPBS programs, tier 3 is for the small proportion of students not responding to tier 1 or tier 2 interventions. It involves intensive, individualized interventions tailored to each student. Small socio-emotional group instruction in social and emotional skills, daily student check-in and check-out procedures, and enlisting family support for small-group intervention and instruction are all techniques associated with tier 2.

45. C: The best action that the principal can take to increase the frequency of classroom observations is to plan the observations into the schedule each week. This will force all other appointments and meetings to be scheduled around the classroom observations. Classroom visits should not be left to chance or they will likely not be conducted due to the many tasks that a principal may have to address throughout the day. Additionally, the principal should aim to visit classrooms on different days of the week and times of the day to obtain a well-rounded perspective of teaching and learning on campus.

46. A: According to some education experts (cf. WestEd.org), school principals and districts surveyed across the United States have reported generally positive impressions of standards-based accountability systems, saying these have improved curriculum and instruction, student assessment practices (C), and student expectations and achievement. However, many districts (over 40%) also reported that teacher morale had been adversely affected by accountability pressures.

47. C: Students designing digital storybooks is the best example of creating content using digital media. It is beneficial for students to access information using technology, such as visiting wiki pages. Students can also curate content that already exists, such as gathering photos from the web. However, creating content using digital media empowers students to use technology at the highest level of Bloom's taxonomy.

48. A: School leaders should not ask students to serve as translators for their parents who do not speak English. Students may be unreliable translators and should not carry the responsibility of translating, especially in matters that the student may not need to be involved in. For parents who have missed school parent workshops, school leaders can record workshops for parents to watch later. They can create inclusive, welcoming, affirming climates by validating, honoring, and thanking family and community members for supporting the school as well as encouraging and maintaining

Copyright © Mometrix Media. You have been licensed one copy of this document for personal use only. Any other reproduction or redistribution is strictly prohibited. All rights reserved.
This content is provided for test preparation purposes only and does not imply an endorsement by Mometrix of any particular political, scientific, or religious point of view.

their meaningful involvement. They can assign parent liaisons, which enable parents to access resources and services that the school offers to families.

49. C: Among school principals' roles in leading the implementation of school-wide technology adoption, prioritizing change and supporting and encouraging faculty (A) are responsibilities associated with the role of motivator and cheerleader. Assuring teachers have what they need to meet change goals (B) is associated with the role of resource provider. Establishing conditions for change by setting standards for learning and collaboration (C) is associated with the role of learning organization leader. Leading change initiatives, resolving problems, and providing learning opportunities for faculty (D) are associated with the role of facilitator.

50. C: The DOJ collaborated with the ED in producing a positive school discipline guidance package as part of the SSDI to prevent or reduce student movement from schools to justice and correctional systems, not match school discipline to practices in those systems; replace disciplinary exclusion with better alternatives, rather than regard student justice involvement as inevitable and wait to address that; ensure Titles IV and VI of the Civil Rights Act prohibiting discrimination are enforced, which is the DOJ's job; and establish fair disciplinary practices to keep all students in school, not exclude any.

51. C: Providing teachers with aggregated student data, even in regular intervals, will not likely improve teacher practice. School leaders must disaggregate data to help teachers identify the data that is reflective of their students and their instructional practice. Disaggregated data should also be analyzed in a collaborative process to help identify needs and generate solutions to address those needs.

52. C: Distributive leadership is a leadership style that shares leadership roles and responsibilities with others in a deliberate and systematic way. Providing team members with leadership opportunities builds capacity and helps to cultivate team members into leaders. Practicing distributive leadership also helps to foster change and improvement because the ideas and talent of team members are leveraged and utilized.

53. B: Reading and writing skills are best taught and reinforced within the context of subject matter content. Creating a cross-curricular focus on reading and writing skills would best address the gap in performance among students who are not reading at grade level. Increasing opportunities for students to read is beneficial, but is less effective in closing opportunity gaps, especially when opportunities to engage in reading are voluntary such as after school or at home. Targeted test preparation has limited efficacy if attendance is voluntary and student performance is not monitored.

54. B: School improvement plans have been found to increase parental meeting and student school attendance; student enrollment and achievement; parental involvement in policies, procedures, advocacy, organizing, and events; and to decrease student behavior problems while increasing student achievement. School system leaders have also established central office policies and structures that increased parental engagement, not only in individual schools but also system-wide.

55. A: Formative data helps teachers to assess their effectiveness during instruction (rather than after) and accordingly make adjustments to improve student outcomes. Summative data can assist teachers in identifying areas of improvement in their teaching practice but is often too late to identify specific remedial student groups. Student profiles from permanent records (e.g., demographics, assessment histories, family information, etc.) provide less detailed information to inform instruction. Enrollment data helps educators identify budgetary needs and student

Copyright © Mometrix Media. You have been licensed one copy of this document for personal use only. Any other reproduction or redistribution is strictly prohibited. All rights reserved.
This content is provided for test preparation purposes only and does not imply an endorsement by Mometrix of any particular political, scientific, or religious point of view.

demographic distributions, but do not inform instruction, staff development, remedial student groups, or information plans.

56. B: Schools and school leaders use data they have collected for setting goals aligned with their school vision and mission. Data-based decision-making is a best practice for school leaders. Data should be collected for all decision making and data can be collected in the forms of quantitative data, such as standardized assessment results, attendance rates, etc., or qualitative data such as survey feedback. School goals must be aligned with the school vision and mission so that progress toward established goals is connected to achieving the school vision and mission.

57. A: The National Education Association (NEA) identifies essential components of any school Acceptable Use Policy (AUP), including a preamble and definition section; an acceptable uses section (B), defining appropriate student internet use; an unacceptable uses section (C), defining prohibited uses, behaviors, and Web sites; a policy statement (D) identifying covered services and student use conditions; and a violation and sanctions section (A) informing students how to question policy applications and report violations, which may conform to the general school disciplinary code.

58. B: Effective induction programs offered by the New Teacher Center and others have impacts on schools of making new teachers more effective, increasing teacher retention rates, strengthening teacher leadership, addressing education inequities, *and* increasing student learning and achievement.

59. D: Students must have rigorous instruction in the classroom to be prepared for challenging curriculum in the future. Students who perform well in class but perform poorly on standardized assessments are evidence of misalignment of course work to standardized assessments or inadequate levels of rigor in the classroom. Evaluating the grades of one grade level of students in a specific class is not evidence of ensuring all students are prepared for a challenging curriculum. Reviewing one assessment that was administered prior to enrollment in the school does not demonstrate ongoing monitoring.

60. B: Students having family issues, or personal problems whose treatment involves family, are referred to family counselors. Group counseling promotes social skills and healthy interaction and can be provided within the school environment when the groups are selected with intention. Career counselors can help students choose career paths and preparation. Career counseling is often performed in schools by guidance counselors and others, making referrals infrequent.

61. D: School principals should remain objective when observing teachers, regardless of their tenure or contract status. An evaluation rubric for teacher assessment should be used fairly and objectively for all teachers. A principal should observe what assignments the teacher gives the students, whether they are actively implementing new strategies, and the overall classroom environment and culture.

62. B: Among resource limitations, inadequate school counselor-to-student ratios are attributable to funding and budget cuts, not accountability mandates. Inadequate in-service development for new support staff is attributable to various factors, including cultural influences stigmatizing mental health issues, lowering their priority in schools; leadership and organizational deficits; and funding deficits, ineffective resource allocation, etc.—not accountability mandates. Inadequate school district mental health budgeting is not federally mandated for accountability. Federal accountability requirements have changed school counselor responsibilities from addressing

Copyright © Mometrix Media. You have been licensed one copy of this document for personal use only. Any other reproduction or redistribution is strictly prohibited. All rights reserved.
This content is provided for test preparation purposes only and does not imply an endorsement by Mometrix of any particular political, scientific, or religious point of view.

student mental health to addressing student academic achievement, reducing professional support services.

63. C: Cooperative learning, the process of facilitating student collaboration, develops social skills, teamwork, individual and collective responsibility, and group interdependence. The Socratic method is useful for facilitating student engagement, assessing student learning, and fostering critical thinking, but is not useful for delivering instruction. Project-based learning is useful for active, hands-on learning experiences and does not require technology to be implemented effectively. Technology is a useful tool for delivering instruction, but is not required; technology is also effective when students utilize technology to engage in the learning process, making technology more student-centered.

64. A: In some states, teachers do not have to be fully certified to teach in a public school. Teachers who are new to the profession and may be enrolled in an alternative teacher certification program may be allowed to teach in a public school on a probationary status. However, all teachers must demonstrate subject-matter competency prior to being deemed highly qualified and able to teach in a public school. States may vary in their requirements for teacher certification; therefore, a teacher who is highly qualified in one state may have to meet additional qualifications if they move to another state.

65. D: The principal should take action that allows stakeholders to participate in the process of refocusing attention to campus vision and goals. A community meeting would allow for two-way communication so that the principal can hear the concerns of the community and so that the community can hear about the alignment of the program to the campus vision and goals.

66. B: Given that students were consistently performing well in math with the exception of three specific math objectives indicates that there is an issue with the curriculum being used to teach those objectives. Factors such as teacher quality or biased assessments would negatively impact student performance in all objectives, not just a select few and performance would vary from student to student. The most likely reason for students consistently underperforming in the same area despite being taught by different teachers is a misalignment of curriculum to the assessment of the objectives.

67. A: Traditionally, bus drivers are considered school support staff, typically under the district Transportation Department. They serve multiple school locations and are usually supervised by an employee in the Transportation Department. Custodians and cafeteria workers are often dedicated to one campus and may be supervised by the campus principal. Volunteers are unpaid and not officially school district employees, but are supervised by the campus principal to ensure compliance with policies and procedures. However, school districts may have differing organizational polices and supervision of campus personnel.

68. D: When school visions are developed through collaboration among employees, they tend to be more appropriate to the contexts of their local school districts, which is an advantage. Collaboratively developed school visions typically are *not* implemented as quickly as those personally developed by school leaders, which also tend to be clearer and more coherent than those developed collaboratively. Collaboratively developed school visions do take longer to develop, slowing change, which is a disadvantage, not an advantage.

69. C: In school change processes, first-order changes represent specific strategies for implementing deeper changes in educational ideas and philosophies. Thus, forming a different instructional approach is a second-order change, as are forming new interactions and relationships

Copyright © Mometrix Media. You have been licensed one copy of this document for personal use only. Any other reproduction or redistribution is strictly prohibited. All rights reserved.
This content is provided for test preparation purposes only and does not imply an endorsement by Mometrix of any particular political, scientific, or religious point of view.

and forming a sense of collaborative ownership among educational stakeholders. For implementing that sense of shared ownership, forming site-based school advisory councils is an example of a corresponding first-order change.

70. A: A school leader should evaluate technology data systems used in the school by how well they provide relevant data for decision making. Affordability and whether other schools are using the data system are important questions to ask when considering purchasing a data system but are less relevant when evaluating the system after use. User friendliness is not as important in evaluation if training and support are readily available to staff who will use the data system.

Constructed Response

1. Essay question graders commonly look for the following elements in a strong response: strong content knowledge, clear organization, and effective arguments or examples. Language and usage are not usually strictly graded, but can make a big impact on the clarity of your ideas.

Please use the provided rubric to make sure your response meets these common criteria. Try to have a friend or family member grade your response for you or take a break after writing your response and return to grade it with fresh eyes.

Constructed Response Rubric

Domain	Description
Content Knowledge	• The response directly addresses every part of the prompt. • The response demonstrates independent knowledge of the topic. • The response discusses the topic at an appropriate depth.
Organization	• The response introduces the topic, usually with a thesis statement or by restating the prompt. • The response directly addresses the prompt by providing a clear and concise answer or solution. • The answer or solution is supported by logical arguments or evidence. • The response restates the main idea in the conclusion.
Arguments and Examples	• The response provides a reasonable answer to the prompt. • The answer is supported by strong reasoning or evidence. • The response develops ideas logically and connects ideas to one another. • The reasoning and evidence provided act to support a unified main idea.
Language and Usage	• The response demonstrates effective use of grammar and uses varied sentence structure throughout the response. • The response demonstrates correct use of spelling, punctuation, and capitalization. • The response demonstrates strong and varied use of vocabulary relevant to the topic and appropriate for the intended audience.

Copyright © Mometrix Media. You have been licensed one copy of this document for personal use only. Any other reproduction or redistribution is strictly prohibited. All rights reserved.
This content is provided for test preparation purposes only and does not imply an endorsement by Mometrix of any particular political, scientific, or religious point of view.

2. Essay question graders commonly look for the following elements in a strong response: strong content knowledge, clear organization, and effective arguments or examples. Language and usage are not usually strictly graded, but can make a big impact on the clarity of your ideas.

Please use the provided rubric to make sure your response meets these common criteria. Try to have a friend or family member grade your response for you or take a break after writing your response and return to grade it with fresh eyes.

Constructed Response Rubric

Domain	Description
Content Knowledge	• The response directly addresses every part of the prompt. • The response demonstrates independent knowledge of the topic. • The response discusses the topic at an appropriate depth.
Organization	• The response introduces the topic, usually with a thesis statement or by restating the prompt. • The response directly addresses the prompt by providing a clear and concise answer or solution. • The answer or solution is supported by logical arguments or evidence. • The response restates the main idea in the conclusion.
Arguments and Examples	• The response provides a reasonable answer to the prompt. • The answer is supported by strong reasoning or evidence. • The response develops ideas logically and connects ideas to one another. • The reasoning and evidence provided act to support a unified main idea.
Language and Usage	• The response demonstrates effective use of grammar and uses varied sentence structure throughout the response. • The response demonstrates correct use of spelling, punctuation, and capitalization. • The response demonstrates strong and varied use of vocabulary relevant to the topic and appropriate for the intended audience.

Copyright © Mometrix Media. You have been licensed one copy of this document for personal use only. Any other reproduction or redistribution is strictly prohibited. All rights reserved.
This content is provided for test preparation purposes only and does not imply an endorsement by Mometrix of any particular political, scientific, or religious point of view.